CALLED

— TO —

COACH

DAILY DEVOTIONS FOR COACHES AND COMPETITORS

CALLED TO COACH

Cross Training Publishing
15418 Weir Street #177
Omaha, NE 68137
(308) 293-3891

DEDICATION

I dedicate this book to my wife, Kathy, my two sons, Jeff and Chris and my parents Gaston and Mary Lee Gee.

Kathy, you are my best friend and constant supporter. What an amazing life we are living and after all these years, you are still the one!

Jeff and Chris, you are truly gifts from the Heavenly Father. You continue to make me proud and I love being your dad.

Gaston and Mary Lee Gee, as my parents you gave me the greatest gifts of all–a love for Jesus Christ and compassion for my fellow man.

FOREWORD

The role of the coach has risen to idolized proportions in our society. American sports are an icon of popularity from the very young to the elderly; more than fifty million adolescents have participated on an athletic team before entering their adult years. In fact, we now spend more time watching, reading or being actively involved in sport activities than any other of life's discretional domains. Because of this cultural focus, the coach has become the point person for this societal phenomenon. In fact, research reflects the coach as one of the most influential persons in American life. The coach now takes on the role of authority figure for many of the traditional American ethos: commitment to goals, team first attitudes, excellence of cause, healthy life attributions, etc. For a variety of reasons, these value systems are being lost or deemphasized in the home environment. It is with this premise that we as sport coaching educators are making a concerted effort to come alongside the coaches' fraternity to help encourage, educate and produce the next generation of coaches to meet the demand of our sport crazed culture.

Because coaches are also teachers, their influence with athletes, in many ways, has lifelong and even eternal impact. Coaches today must have inspired resources to help them meet changing expectations on and off the field.

The role and influence of the coach is now a central focus of the international sport ministry organization, the Fellowship of Christian Athletes (FCA) and its 3Dimensional Coach teaching/learning strategies. It is a visual reference for coaches to identify their coaching style (philosophy) as related to Biblical principles and accentuated by current research. This book, written by a 'coach for coaches,' is an ideal companion of infusing God's playbook with the daily integration for the coaching life. Each devotion is timely, relevant and spot on for today's coaches. I have been so blessed by reading each one. The infusion of these devotions in the coach's life will be a beginning or continuing personal transformational process of the coach to gain or enhance the joy of being "Called to Coach."

It is a joy to witness the coach and his/her family fulfilling God's purpose to be a great coach with an even greater message! Thank you Coach Gee for creating such a great resource for us coaches!

INTRODUCTION

Somewhere on this crazy journey called coaching, my perspective changed. I still loved the game, I loved the competition and I recognized I didn't want to be anywhere else. I enjoyed the smells and the sounds that go with the games. I never grew tired of seeing timid young boys and girls grow into young men and women with great determination and self-confidence. What changed was that I began to look at why I coached instead of how I coached. I began to see coaching as a calling rather than a job; I realized I was doing something I loved and making a difference in the lives of others at the same time. It hit me that God had made me the way I am, and He had called me to coach. When I grasped the answer to why I coach, the how I coached changed too.

Therein lies the motivation for this book. I know there are many coaches who also see coaching as a calling. To those who are not there yet, I hope to challenge you to look at your why. I understand that coaches are very busy people; it doesn't matter what level you coach, your time is a valuable resource. The duties and responsibilities that accompany coaching are demanding and never-ending. Beyond the Xs and Os, coaches must make decisions regarding motivation, team cohesion and how to instill confidence in their athletes. Coaching can be a 24/7 challenge that pulls us away from our families, our friendships and our faith. Where can the busy coach go for a fresh outlook on the profession and to search for his or her why? For the coach wanting to go deeper in their faith, is there anything available that can help take them there? It was with those questions in mind that I began the journey to provide hope and encouragement for the people I love and respect the most–coaches.

Coaches spend countless hours perfecting their skills. We go to clinics, watch video, read books and pick the brains of fellow coaches every time we have the chance. We are always looking for that one take-away to give us an edge on the competition. While those methods can be effective, I believe God has provided us with an amazing blueprint for our profession and our lives, His Word. The Bible contains the answer to every question a coach or competitor can ask. These devotions are short and to the point. I know how busy you are, but I want to challenge you and inspire you to go deeper into God's Word. My desire is that this decision will change your life like it has mine. As coaches and competitors, we must always be learning and growing. We must do the same in our faith. Enjoy the journey.

Pursue and Persist

"But Jesus called them over and said, 'You know that the rulers of the Gentiles dominate them, and the men of high position exercise power over them. It must not be like that among you. On the contrary, whoever wants to become great among you must be your servant, and whoever wants to be first among you must be your slave; just as the Son of Man did not come to be served, but to serve, and to give His life–a ransom for many.'" Matthew 20:25-28

Motivation could be defined as "the inclination to pursue and persist." In simple terms, that means to "get after it" and "stay after it." It's more difficult than ever to motivate athletes. It's harder to get players to come out and stay out. Players will quit in a heartbeat. If asked why, the replies include too much work, being burned out or not having fun. They miss practice, they give up when the team starts struggling, and they complain about wanting more touches and playing time. As coaches, we know all about the Xs and Os. We know that having the "Jimmy's and Joe's" is important too. We must explore new ways to get athletes out and keep them out. Many coaches are finding a better way. They're taking time to build relationships with their athletes, and they are getting to know them on and off the field. They're learning to be servant leaders.

Jesus had some challenges with His team too. The disciples all wanted to be great, and Jesus seized the opportunity to explain what it takes to be great. He told them their thinking was misguided. Greatness is not about having more knowledge or being in a position of authority. Jesus explained that in His Kingdom things would be different. The ticket to greatness is service. Whoever wants to be great must first become a servant to others. God has not put us in our coaching positions with the sole purpose of mastering the Xs and Os and winning games. He wants us to make an eternal difference in the lives of the young men and women we coach. Jesus calls us not only to coach them but also to serve them.

Father, thank You for sending Your Son Jesus, to model how to serve others. Teach us to be servant leaders. Use us in powerful ways to make a difference for eternity. Amen.

Don't Quit

"So I say to you, keep asking, and it will be given to you. Keep searching, and you will find. Keep knocking, and the door will be opened to you. For everyone who asks receives, and the one who searches finds, and to the one who knocks, the door will be opened." Luke 11:9-10

When I was forty-four years old, I ran my first marathon, the Marine Corps Marathon in Washington, D.C. I'm not sure why I did it; maybe it was part of a midlife crisis. I think I wanted to prove to myself that I could do it. Many of my friends thought I was crazy, and maybe I was to think I could run 26.2 miles. I joined the Leukemia Society's *Team in Training* program, and they taught me how to train properly. Six months of training built my endurance as well as my confidence. It was hard, and there were no shortcuts. If I didn't do the work, there would be little chance of finishing the race. I have heard the marathon described as two races, the first 20 miles and the last 6.2 miles. The last 6.2 miles were painful, and I remember wanting to quit. When I crossed the finish line, I was overcome with emotion realizing I had done something I didn't think I could do.

In our Scripture, Luke is teaching us not to get discouraged or quit in our prayer life. Sometimes God answers our prayers the first time we ask, and in other cases, He answers only after prolonged asking. We are to keep asking, keep searching, and keep knocking. Luke is reminding us that everyone who asks receives; everyone who seeks finds, and everyone who knocks, has it opened to him. When we pray, God always gives us what we ask or He gives us something better. A no answer means that He knows our request would not be the best for us, and His denial is better than our request. As coaches, we are always telling our players not to quit. Our challenge is to follow our own advice when it comes to prayer. Don't quit; God answers prayer.

Thank You Father for always being available when I need to talk with You. Give me the strength to keep going today, even when I want to quit. Amen.

A Solid Foundation

"For we are God's co-workers. You are God's field, God's building. According to God's grace that was given to me, as a skilled master builder I have laid a foundation, and another builds on it, because no one can lay any other foundation than what has been laid—that is, Jesus Christ." 1 Corinthians 3:9-11

Most sports begin with building a strong base. In baseball, it's pitching; in football, it's blocking and tackling, and in weight training, it's using the proper technique. Success in sports is all about building a solid foundation. Successful coaches know what it takes to achieve success. We must keep in mind, however, that it's possible to build the wrong kind of base or to have no base at all. Some baseball teams think they can win with good hitting alone, but as the season wears on, they find out their pitching isn't good enough. A football team might put a flashy offense on the field but be unable to stop anyone on defense. A weightlifter who focuses too much on how much weight he is lifting but neglects proper technique is likely to get injured.

People, like sports teams, can make the mistake of building their lives on the wrong foundation. Then, when trouble comes our way, our lives crumble around us. What we thought was a strong foundation built on money, relationships, or good deeds did not hold up when the going got tough. The Apostle Paul taught the Christians of Corinth that the only true foundation was Jesus Christ. Suddenly, it seemed someone had presented the people with conflicting foundations.vIn 1 Corinthians 3:11, Paul is reminding the people of Corinth not to build their lives on anything other than Jesus. We too can be fooled by the "good things," and the thought that these things can bring us security. We must remember that only one foundation is needed for a building, and we are God's house. We must build our lives on Jesus because nothing else will last.

Thank You Father for being the Rock of my life. Teach me today that You are all I need. Amen.

Endurance

"Therefore since we also have such a large cloud of witnesses surrounding us, let us lay aside every weight and the sin that so easily ensnares us, and run with endurance the race that lies before us, keeping our eyes on Jesus, the source and perfecter of our faith....." Hebrews 12:1-2

Endurance. In life and coaching, we know the importance of endurance. As a track coach, I learned to appreciate the difficulty of each event, but I was especially drawn to the distance athlete. It takes a special person to train and compete in the longer races. Endurance athletes require a great deal of discipline, and they must be able to stay focused on their goals. I have always been fascinated by the athletes who compete in the Ironman Triathlons. To be able to swim, bike and run long distances in the same event is truly a testimony to the strength of the human body. Years ago, I had the opportunity to serve as a volunteer at a local sprint triathlon. While the distances are shorter than the Ironman Triathlon, they still require tremendous endurance. It was my privilege to meet Jason during that event. Jason had been seriously injured in a motorcycle accident and paralyzed below his chest. I was asked to help Jason transition from the swim portion of the race to his bike. That experience encouraged me and humbled me at the same time. Jason's inner strength and endurance was an inspiration to me as well as those who watched him compete.

Following Jesus can be tough at times. It can be difficult to stay strong in our faith with all of the distractions that surround us. It's important to remember that we are never going through the tough time alone. Jesus will run the race with us if we let Him. While we don't know the distance of our race, focusing on Him will give us the strength to reach the finish line. We must continue to work on building our spiritual endurance. We can do that by spending time in His Word and talking to Him on our knees.

Thank You Heavenly Father for always being with me, in the tough times and in the good times. Help me today to run my race with strength and endurance. Amen.

100%

"Do you not know that the runners in a stadium all race, but only one receives the prize? Run in such a way that you may win." 1 Corinthians 9:24

100%. As coaches, we are always asking our athletes to give their all when they compete. Rarely do we get it! As a young track coach, I can remember having my athletes run laps as part of their training. There was a section of the route that went behind a building, and I would lose sight of the runners for a brief time. It didn't take long for me to realize some of the athletes would take advantage of that situation and walk when out of my watchful eye. On one occasion, I even caught two runners hiding behind the building waiting for the other runners to come back around, cutting off a complete lap. To give 100% has a cost most are not willing to pay. Athletes who take shortcuts, are lazy or halfhearted in their efforts, seldom reach the finish line first. To win takes every ounce of an athlete's heart, body and soul.

Paul reminds us that the Christian life is like a race. To win takes effort. He knew many Corinthians had attended the Isthmian Games near Corinth and were familiar with athletic events. He is telling them that they must do everything in their power to share the good news of Jesus Christ. He took a job on the side so he could preach. He did whatever was needed to win people to the Lord. These efforts often resulted in hardship, but Paul was determined to give 100% to the call God had given him. He was running with everything he had and his eyes were on the finish line, not what was going on around him. Are you giving God 100% or settling for a halfhearted effort? Are you running for the prize, or are you content just to be in the race?

Lord, I want to give 100% today because You gave Your all for me. Amen.

Special Teams

"Whatever you do, do it enthusiastically, as something done for the Lord, and not for men." Colossians 3:23

It takes a different mindset to get on the football field as part of a special teams unit. These guys are often viewed as fanatics, reckless and out of control. Coaches refer to special-teams players as head-hunters and designate athletes as gunners whose job it is to race downfield and be the first man to tackle the ball carrier. You can't "dog it" and be part of the special team. Coaches are always looking for ways to motivate these players. Old Dominion University special-teams coach Mike Zyskowski awarded dog tags as rewards for superior play. Each tag is inscribed with the words, Special Ops. Zyskowski says, "To get one, you have to demonstrate everything we as coaches want out of a special-team player." To the casual fan, a special-teams player may not seem as glamorous as quarterback or linebacker, but coaches know they can be the difference in winning and losing games.

In Colossians 3:23, Paul reminds us whatever the role God has given us to play, we must carry it out to the best of our ability. Sometimes in our everyday life, we are asked to do things that seem trivial and unimportant. As part of God's team, we must remember every job is important. No task is too small or insignificant in God's eyes. When we humble ourselves and recognize that we are doing it for the Lord, the picture changes. Rewards in heaven will not be based on our perceived success or talents but our faithfulness. We are all special in God's eyes. Whatever God has called you to do, do it enthusiastically.

Father, help me understand that everything I do today has significance. Guide me as I complete the small stuff and the big stuff in life. Amen.

Pressing On

"Not that I have already reached (the goal) or am already fully mature, but I make every effort to take hold of it because I also have been taken hold of by Jesus Christ." Philippians 3:12

Every year, the NFL draft takes center stage in the world of sports. College players from across the country wait to hear their names called and realize the dream that only a handful of athletes can experience. Years of hard work can translate into millions of dollars in an instant. For months, the gifts and talents of these young men are evaluated under the watchful eyes of scouts and analysts. How fast are they; are they big enough; do they have the right mental make-up; is he worthy of being a first-round pick or will he fall to a later round? It's not unusual to hear comments like "he has a strong arm, but he must work on his release," or "he is gifted physically, but he will have to become a better pass blocker." Somewhere in the process, athletes realize that even the best college players have to continue working hard to stay in the NFL. Someone once said, "Satisfaction is the grave of progress." How easy it is to stay where we are. We tell ourselves we have worked hard and deserve to take it easy for a little while. Or we convince ourselves we are doing better than most everyone else we know. When we allow ourselves to stop growing, we are standing on a slippery slope.

The life of the Apostle Paul is certainly worthy of imitating. Paul was more than willing to suffer and die for his Lord and Savior Jesus Christ, yet he never considered himself perfect. He knew he had more work to do to become everything God wanted him to be. He had to continue pressing on! As coaches we may be winning games, but are we making a positive difference in the lives of those young men and women God has placed in our care? We may be a good person, but are we truly striving to be who God is calling us to be? The Christian race has no finish line. We must continue striving and straining to become more Christ-like each day.

Heavenly Father, help me keep pressing on today. Keep me hungry as I strive to know You more. Amen.

Grace

"For all have sinned and fall short of the glory of God." Romans 3:23

How often have we heard the statement, "Sports not only teaches us about winning and losing, it teaches us about life?" Perfection in the sports arena is rare. Two men, Detroit Tiger pitcher's, Armando Galarraga and Major League umpire Jim Joyce, met on center stage and the world witnessed a remarkable example of good sportsmanship. Galarraga needed one more out to complete a perfect game. On a ground ball fielded by the first baseman, Galarraga sprinted from the mound to cover first base and stepped on the bag a fraction of a second before the runner made contact. Time stood still as players and fans began to celebrate. What happened next changed the lives of both Galarraga and Joyce. Jim Joyce called the runner safe. Galarraga looked at the umpire with a smile, went back to the mound and recorded the final out. Following the game, Joyce watched the tape and realized he had missed the call. He faced reporters and admitted his mistake. He asked to speak with Galarraga. Upset and in tears, Joyce hugged the pitcher and said, "You were perfect; I was not." Galarraga and Joyce chose to focus on humility and grace rather than the mistake. Galarraga responded, "He was wrong and apologized; what can I do about that?"

It's refreshing to see someone take responsibility for a mistake, apologize and be forgiven. God wants that to happen in our lives too. Only God is perfect! Our imperfection separates us from God, but because He loves us, He has provided a solution to the problem. Jesus Christ, God's only Son, died on a cross as a substitute for our sin. When we confess our sins to God and accept Jesus Christ as our Savior and Lord, we are forgiven and become God's children forever. God is a God of grace. You may find it ironic that in a recent ESPN survey of major league players, Jim Joyce was ranked as baseball's #1 umpire.

Lord Jesus, I need You. I'm a sinner and need Your forgiveness. You loved me so much that You died on the cross for my sins and rose from the dead. I repent of my sins and put my faith in You. Take control of my life and help me to follow You in obedience. Amen.

Focus

"Therefore, all who are mature should think this way. And if you think differently about anything, God will reveal this to you also." Philippians 3:15

Who can forget the eyes? When thinking of focus and intensity on the football field, Mike Singletary should be on everyone's short list. His nicknames, Samurai Mike and Iron Mike, helped create an image few have matched while playing in the National Football League. Singletary spent his entire twelve-year career playing linebacker for the Chicago Bears. Ten times he was named to the Pro Bowl; he is listed as one of the top 100 football players of all time and was inducted into the Pro Football Hall of Fame in 1998. Singletary once said, "I didn't just want to play football–*I had to play!*" He loved the game and was willing to do whatever it took to play. His desire to be the best helped him overcome childhood sickness, a broken home and being raised poor. Mike Singletary played football with passion and focus.

When it comes to the desire to know and follow Jesus Christ, the Apostle Paul would be on everyone's short list. Paul was devoted to God and is remembered as one of the strongest defenders of the Christian faith. Someone said that no other person in the Bible, aside from Christ Himself, had a more lasting influence on his world or ours. Paul was tough, tenacious, and relentless in his passion for Jesus. His courage was unwavering in the face of personal hardship and danger. Where did Paul's focus come from? It came from an intense desire to thank God for His undeserved grace. Paul's life serves as a source of hope for us all. God can use people of passion and focus. When we focus on Jesus and strive to follow His model for life, we too can be used by God to accomplish great things.

Lord, I want to be passionate for You today as I strive to be all You have called me to be. I know I can accomplish great things in Your strength. Amen.

Making Memories

"Our steps were closely followed, so that we could not walk in our streets. Our end drew near; our time ran out. Our end had come!" Lamentations 4:18

When Kenny Chesney released his hit *"The Boys of Fall"* it stirred up some great memories of playing high school football. Growing up in a small rural South Carolina town, fall Friday nights were something special. Like yesterday, I can see the bleachers filled with cheering classmates and family members. I remember "Doc" Thomas passing the hat shouting, "we have to feed those boys, they played a great game!" The smells of popcorn from the canteen and sweat-filled locker rooms are still fresh in my mind. The song's lyrics cut me to the core.

> *When I feel that chill, smell that fresh cut grass,*
> *I'm back in my helmet, cleats and shoulder pads.*
> *Standing in the huddle listening to the call,*
> *Fans going crazy for the boys of fall.*
> *They didn't just let anybody in that club,*
> *Took every ounce of heart and sweat and blood.*
> *To get to wear those game jerseys down the hall,*
> *Kings of the school man, we're the boys of fall.*

Little did I realize the value of making memories as I played high school athletics, and I tear up thinking about the relationships that developed through the experience. Lamentations 4:18 reminds each of us that our time on this earth is limited. A question we must ask ourselves with regularity is, "Am I using my time wisely?" Am I making good memories between my team, my family, and my friends, memories that will last a lifetime? Each of us will stand before God when our time on earth is done. He's not likely to ask, "How many games did you win," but rather, "What kind of father/mother were you; what kind of friend were you;" or "what kind of son/daughter were you?" It's not too late; make a memory today.

Heavenly Father, help me live in the moment and make wonderful memories today. Amen.

Role Model

"Likewise, encourage the young men to be sensible about everything. Set an example of good works yourself, with integrity and dignity in your teaching. Your message is to be sound beyond reproach, so that the opponent will be ashamed, having nothing bad to say about us." Titus 2:6-8

Jim Kleckley was a gifted athlete in his youth, having lettered in three high school sports and received an athletic scholarship to attend college. At 17, he signed a professional baseball contract with the Baltimore Orioles but one year later enlisted in the U.S. Navy to serve his country in World War II. Following his discharge, Jim continued his professional baseball career for nine seasons as a pitcher with the Pittsburgh Pirates and the Cleveland Indians. That's a great athletic resume, but what I saw in Jim Kleckley's life goes much deeper than sports. Jim was married for 62 years and raised three children; he got up and went to work every day with an attitude of joy and commitment. He loved to hunt and fish, and he poured into others through youth baseball, prison ministry, and the Fellowship of Christian Athletes. Jim loved his church, being around people, and talking about Jesus. Jim Kleckley was a true role model.

When spending time with Jim Kleckley, the subject of sports seldom came up. Jim was always friendly and fun to be around. He never talked down to me or preached to me. It was obvious Jim loved and cared about people, and when I was around him, I knew he loved and cared about me. He just lived his life, and I watched. Do you wonder where the next generation is picking up the lessons they need for life? Who is going to fill that void? Remember, everyone is a role model, but not everyone is a positive role model. You have a platform that is unique to you; remember that and like Jim Kleckley, change lives around you.

Father, help me be a positive influence on the lives of others today. Amen.

Who Can You Depend On?

"Be satisfied with what you have, for I will never leave you or forsake you."
Hebrews 13:5

To those who follow college football, Coach Tom Osborne is a legend. He coached the Nebraska Cornhuskers from 1973 to 1997, compiling a record of 255-49-3. That means his teams won more than 83% of their games! When coaches have that kind of success over that length of time, I give them credit for knowing what they're doing. Coach Osborne had a sign in the Nebraska football locker room that read as follows:

> *"Even though we have been good in other years, this year holds no*
> *guarantee of success.*
> *Success doesn't come automatically.*
> *Fans are fans. Some will stick with you, some won't.*
> *The only people who really understand, the ones you can count on*
> *beyond a doubt, who will be with you whether you are 8-and-3 or 3-*
> *and-8,*
> *Are the people in THIS room!"*

Coach Osborne wanted his players to know that their success would not be determined by the accomplishments of previous Nebraska teams. He wanted them to understand the fickle loyalty of fans yet remember the importance of staying united as teammates. In sports and life, we are often confronted with the question, "Who can we depend on?" In Hebrews 13:5, we find an answer we can rely on regardless of the circumstances we might find ourselves in. Jesus promises that He will never abandon us nor will He give up on us. Never means, "at no time" and "not in any circumstance." Has anyone ever made that kind of commitment to you? What a friend we have in Jesus, and through Him, we too can have that kind of assurance.

Heavenly Father, help me today to know that I can always depend on You.
Others may quit on me or disappoint me, but You never will. Amen.

True Success

"His master said to him, 'Well done, good and faithful slave! You were faithful over a few things; I will put you in charge of many things. Share your master's joy!'" Matthew 25:21

In coaching and life, our perspective on success often changes as we gain experience. That's probably just a nice way of saying we get smarter as we get older. One of the true success stories in high school football belongs to Coach Roger Barta and the Redmen of Smith Center, Kansas. Coach Barta is a legend in western Kansas and became known across the country as his teams put together a 79-game win streak and won five straight state championships from 2004-2008. When asked about his coaching philosophy Coach Barta said, "Respect each other, then learn to love each other, and together we are champions." While winning football games is important to Barta, he emphasizes to his players and community the importance of working hard and getting a little better each day, both as an athlete and as a person.

Success is defined as "the peace of mind that comes from knowing you did your best to become the best you are capable of becoming." When we first begin coaching, winning is so important. If we aren't careful, we can let the scoreboard consume us and those we coach. Coach Barta's definition of success is to raise the town's children well and send kids into life who know that every day means something. The Apostle Paul gave everything he had to every task. Yes, he stumbled at times, but he didn't quit, drop out or give up. His faith never wavered. He worked hard and got a little bit better each day. When his life was finished, he heard the words we all hope to hear one day, "Well done, good and faithful servant!" Now that is true success.

Heavenly Father, help me see success as You see it. Teach me Lord, to go beyond the scoreboard and to grasp the much bigger task You have called me to. Amen.

Running the Plays

"Through the proof of this service, they will glorify God for your obedience to the confession of the gospel of Christ and for your generosity in sharing with them and with others." 2 Corinthians 9:13

Imagine yourself at a football game. You watch the offensive team huddle and call the play to be executed against the waiting defense. After a few seconds, all the players clap their hands and yell "break" in unison, but instead of going to the line of scrimmage and running the play, the entire team goes to the sideline and sits down on the bench. What thoughts would go through your mind if you witnessed such an unlikely scenario? The players were properly equipped and certainly looked ready to play. Surely the coaches had taught them how to execute the play that was called. All the players appeared to be confident and excited when they broke the huddle together. What happened? Why didn't they go to the line of scrimmage and run the play?

While it's unlikely we'll see this situation happen at a football game; we see it happen too frequently in our personal lives. We are properly equipped and ready for action with our Bibles in hand. The pastor calls a great play, and some of us clap our hands and shout "Amen." We are confident and excited as we file out of the church and head to the parking lot. However, with the coming of Monday morning, we get up, head for the sidelines and sit down on the bench. What happened? Why didn't we go run the play? With Christ in us, we are expected to run the plays, not sit on the sidelines. When we are obedient to God and execute the plays He has called us to run, we honor Him. God wants us to get into the game and get dirty! He wants us in action, not watching everyone else play.

Lord, help me today to get off the sidelines and into the game. Help me understand that when I am obedient, we can execute amazing plays together. Amen.

What Are You Teaching?

"Not many should become teachers, my brothers, knowing that we will receive a stricter judgment." James 3:1

Regardless of the level of competition, sports are a big deal. Unfortunately, the line between healthy competition and winning at all costs becomes more blurred with each passing year. I heard a distressing story recently from a disheartened softball mom. Her daughter's high school team participated in a weekend tournament with teams from across the state. In a very close contest with a local rival, it was discovered that the opponent was using "mush balls" when the daughter's team was batting. The balls were well used and more suitable for practice than competition. When the opponent took their turn at the plate, quality balls were put in play, creating a significant advantage. The most distressing part of the story is that the rival coach was doing this intentionally.

Great coaches are also great teachers! Obviously, what this coach was teaching was not worth learning. While James 3:1 specifically applies to teaching the word of God, I don't believe it's a stretch to apply this verse to our role as coaches. Coaches are given a significant platform to influence their athletes positively or negatively. It's important that we not take our position as a teacher lightly. Teachers have a place of great responsibility, and what we teach has far-reaching effects. We can never expect to lead others beyond what we have practiced. Teachers can shape others into their image. Coaches who cheat are teaching their athletes to cheat. Coaches who are responsible, fair, and stress good sportsmanship are instilling those same values in their players. Coaching is a high calling; how are you measuring up?

Heavenly Father, give me wisdom today as I lead those You have entrusted to me. I pray I will always be a person of integrity. Amen.

Go to Work!

"There is profit in all hard work, but endless talk leads only to poverty."
Proverbs 14:23

A battered lunch pail has long served as the trademark of Virginia Tech's rough-and-tough style of defensive football. It represents the blue-collar work ethic the Hokies adopted long ago, as they transformed from a doormat into one of the most consistent programs in college football. "What that lunch pail is about is going out and earning success and deserving victory, whatever it is, whether, it's on the field or off the field," says Bud Foster, who started the lunch pail tradition after he was named Virginia Tech's defensive coordinator in 1995. For years, Foster has awarded the lunch pail to the team's defensive MVP from the previous week's game. Too often, in the world of sports and life, we forget the value of good old fashioned hard work! We hear the talk, but we don't see the walk.

God tells us that all honorable work is profitable, but talk without action leads only to poverty. Do you know anyone who talks about their problems for hours but never lifts a finger to solve them? Coach Foster also chose the lunch pail because it represented the work ethic and pride of the working class community living in the foothills of the Blue Ridge Mountains near the Virginia Tech campus. It takes hard work to get things done. "Get up, pack your lunch, and go to work!" What a simple but profound approach to coaching, as well as life.

Lord, help me not to be afraid of hard work. Too often I call out to You for help yet am not willing to do my part. Father help me today to get up, pack my lunch, and go to work! Amen.

118 – 24

"This is the day the Lord has made; let us rejoice and be glad in it."
Psalm 118:24

In his book *InsideOut Coaching*, Joe Ehrmann tells the story of a struggling Syracuse University lacrosse team that was down by a score of 7-3 at halftime. It was an away game being played in the rain, and many of the players were suffering from the flu. The players expected a tough halftime speech from Coach Roy Simmons, Jr. As they waited, soaking wet and exhausted, Coach Simmons simply stood in the locker room looking at them. Then, he went to the chalkboard and wrote in big, bold figures **118-24!** Turning to face his players, Coach Simmons looked each player in the eye and smiled. What could it possibly mean? Was this a new play to be used in the second half? "Psalm 118, verse 24. 'This is the day that the Lord has made, let us rejoice and be glad in it.'" "That's it, men. Win, lose or draw; ENJOY! Let's get back out there and play like you love the game and each other." Syracuse dominated the second half!

What a great lesson! Sports are meant to be enjoyed regardless of the score. Sports are a gift and an honor to play. Sports foster a satisfying sense of community. When you enjoy what you're doing and enjoy who you're doing it with, team performance automatically improves. A tradition was born that day. Players continue to post the numbers **118-24** on the chalkboard year after year.

Heavenly Father, thank You for the opportunity to play the game. Help me grasp the awesomeness of playing a game I love with the people I love to be with. Lord, help me rejoice in this day which is a gift from You. Amen.

Adversity

"A friend loves at all times, and a brother is born for a difficult time."
Proverbs 17:17

In the world of sports, things change quickly. Momentum can shift on a single play. The excitement and cheers of a fan can suddenly turn to disappointment and tears. What appears to be certain victory can be snatched away in mere seconds. Every athlete, coach, and fan knows adversity is inevitable, but that doesn't make it easier when it happens to our athlete or our team. During the 2011 season, the University of North Carolina basketball team was celebrating an 87-73 victory over Creighton in the third round of the NCAA Midwest Regional. Players were confident as they spoke about moving on to St. Louis for the regional finals. Then Coach Roy Williams walked into the locker room and announced that point guard Kendall Marshall had fractured his wrist during the game. The joyful locker room suddenly grew quiet as Marshall's teammates began processing the news. You could see the questions on their faces. Will Marshall be able to play? If he can't play, how will it impact the team? Who will replace him?

Things can change quickly in our lives too. Illness, a tragic accident or difficult relationships can turn our lives upside down. Everything is right with the world and then "Wham!" It's often during the hard times that we find out who our friends are. True friends will be there and stand with us. True friends love in adversity as well as in prosperity. Proverbs 17:17 gives us great encouragement. Brothers are born for adversity; they are at our side when we need them the most. Jesus is like that too. Johnson Outman describes Jesus' love this way: "There's not an hour He is not near us. No, not one! No, not one! No night so dark but His love can cheer us, No, not one! No, not one!" Oh, what a friend we have in Jesus!!!

Heavenly Father, help us understand that adversity comes with life. Surround us with caring teammates and friends who walk with us in the good times and bad. Teach us to be that kind of teammate and friend to others. Thank you Father for showing us love through Your Son Jesus, who You promise will never leave us. Amen.

Driving Lesson

"When you walk, your steps will not be hindered; when you run, you will not stumble." Proverbs 4:12

Baseball is full of colorful characters! At the top of anyone's list of unique players, You would likely find the name Yogi Berra. The New York Yankee catcher had the unique ability to say things that didn't make sense, yet everyone seemed to understand exactly what he was saying. Once when driving with his wife, Carmen, and their three sons, Berra got lost. Carmen was giving him a hard time about it when Yogi suddenly blurted out, "We may be lost, but we're making good time!" Now that's a statement I can relate to. As a coach, it's easy to find ourselves working extremely hard and putting in long hours to reach a destination that has not even been determined. Does this make any sense?

God's Word tells us He has a definite plan and destination for our lives. Have you ever found yourself heading in the wrong direction, or to an unknown destination, but making good time? How often do we wind up in the blind alleys and take the wrong turns in our daily lives? Solomon's wise counsel reminds us of two very important principles. First, God wants to guide us step by step. To be blunt, God wants to do the driving! Second, God guides people when they are moving toward Him. A ship must be in motion before the captain can steer it. The same is true of us. God will guide us when we are in motion toward Him. Move over and let God get behind the wheel. You'll find the drive more enjoyable, and the destination will be heavenly.

Lord, forgive me for always wanting to drive. You know where I need to go and the best way for me to get there. Teach me, Lord, to move over and let You do the driving. Amen.

Thanks Mom!

"I am teaching you the way of wisdom; I am getting you on straight paths."
Proverbs 4:11

Mother's Day is special! Though my mother is no longer physically alive, she is very much alive in my heart. She had a tremendous influence on my life, and I am grateful for everything she did to make me a better person. One of the things I remember most was her patience with my love for sports. We spent hours discussing the batting averages of my favorite baseball players. She lovingly sewed number 44 on the football jersey I received for Christmas one year so I could wear the same number as my professional football hero. Mom was as excited as I was when we made our annual summer trip to see the Atlanta Braves play. I don't know if mom loved sports, but I do know she loved me. She willingly gave her time and support to the things I enjoyed. We talked endlessly about sports, but we also talked a great deal about the things that are important in life. She shared her wisdom and helped keep me on the right path during my youth.

As coaches, we too have countless opportunities to teach wisdom and guide our athletes along the right path. Are we making the most of them? Are we making ourselves available when they come to us seeking answers to difficult questions? Are we concerned about their spiritual development as much as we are their athletic development? Are we there for them when they need a helping hand and encouragement? While winning will always be important, so is being a positive influence, a good listener, and a spiritual leader to those we serve. Do we love our players? Are we looking solely at the physical gifts and talents of our athletes, or are we looking at them the way God looks at us all, with love?

Heavenly Father, thank You for mothers and all those who have poured themselves into our lives. Teach us to be better encouragers, better listeners and better leaders to those in our care. Teach us to love others in the same way You love us. Amen.

Classic or Clunker?

"Do you not know that your body is a sanctuary of the Holy Spirit who is in you, whom you have from God? You are not your own, for you were bought at a price; therefore glorify God in your body." 1 Corinthians 6:19-20

What if you could buy any car you wanted? Let's say you decided on a Ferrari; how would you treat it? My guess is that you would clean it every day, keep it tuned properly, and burn only the best fuel. Using the proper fuel in an expensive sports car is important. A Ferrari requires a certain burning ratio to the fuel, and if abused over time, the engine will suffer a loss of power and a shorter lifespan. Which do you think is worth more–a Ferrari or your body? Do you think you're worth the time and energy it takes to keep your body running at a high level? Think of your body as treasure. The better you take care of yourself on a mental and physical level the more rewards you will receive. Also, you may also notice that others are treating you better. This is because when you take care of yourself, you are sending a message to the world as well as yourself that you are worth it!

What does the engine God gave you need? First, it needs proper rest. Rest relieves stress, recharges our energy sources, and improves our mental awareness. Second, we need exercise. Exercise helps improve our mental attitude and reduce stress, allowing us to rest better. Third, we need to pay attention to the fuel we're putting into our engine. Fast food and junk food aren't what our human engines need to run efficiently. Balanced meals and better eating habits will make you feel, look, and think better. God gave us our bodies, and the Holy Spirit lives there. We're commanded to take care of ourselves. God says, "we are not our own." It's not up to us to take our bodies and use them any way we want. We must treat our bodies as a temple or holy place. If God has made our body to perform like a Ferrari, we should not treat it like a Ford Pinto.

Heavenly Father, help me remember that one of my greatest gifts is good health. Amen.

Impact Player

"You did not choose Me, but I chose you. I appointed you that you should go out and produce fruit and that your fruit should remain, so that whatever you ask the Father in My name, He will give you." John 15:16

Reading Bobby Richardson's book, *Impact Player, Leaving a Lasting Legacy On & Off the Field,* has given me the chance to travel back in time. The journey is filled with simple memories of childhood and a growing love for the game of baseball. In 1960, my grandfather gave the family an amazing gift, our first television. On Saturdays, my baseball education began when I discovered something called *the Game of the Week.* More times than not, the New York Yankees were playing, and I immediately became a Yankee fan. Bobby Richardson, from my home state of South Carolina, played second base. The Yankees of that era became one of the greatest dynasties in baseball history. Through the years, my respect for Richardson grew, because I came to realize he was the glue that held those great teams together. Richardson was an outstanding baseball player, but his greatest claim to fame is the way he has lived his life. Richardson says, "my aim in both baseball and life has been simple: to make an impact by being used by God in the lives of others."

We can easily become discouraged in our Christian walk. Jesus knew this and reminded His disciples that not only had He chosen them but He would give them whatever they needed to get the job done. Like Richardson, Jesus is calling each of us to be "impact players." This is a long, difficult journey that takes time but can produce wonderful fruit. It's important to remember, however, that we can't do the job by ourselves. While God does His part, we must provide the patience, persistence, and prayer.

Father, thank You for providing everything I need to be an impact player for You. Give me the strength for the journey. Amen.

Coach Ed Thomas

"I have told you these things so that in Me you may have peace. You will have suffering in this world. Be courageous! I have conquered the world." John 16:33

As coaches, we know about trouble. Trouble can come in many forms: an undisciplined athlete, an unfair referee, a difficult parent or an unreasonable principal. Trouble seems to come with the territory. Why is it that some people focus on the opportunity trouble brings, while others focus on the problem? In his book *The Sacred Acre*, Mark Tabb tells the incredible story of Coach Ed Thomas of Parkersburg, Iowa. On a Sunday in May 2008, an F5 tornado struck the town destroying 250 homes and businesses in thirty-five seconds. The next day, Coach Thomas made an amazing prediction "God willing, we will play our first home game here on this field this season." One hundred days later, the Falcons won on the field they called "the Sacred Acre" and inspired a town to come together to rebuild the hurting community. This powerful story is a testimony of how one man's attitude led others to take trouble and turn it on its head.

Jesus teaches us a great deal about troubles. He warns us that life is not easy; difficulty and suffering come with the territory. "You will have suffering," Jesus told his disciples. Like a wonderful friend, Jesus does not leave us to battle our troubles alone. He invites us to experience the peace of His presence. "I will never leave you or forsake you," Jesus promises. With that promise, Jesus offers us the choice to walk in our troubles alone or in peace with Him. Like the church sign says, "Know Jesus, Know Peace; No Jesus, No Peace."

Father, I don't like when trouble comes my way, but I am grateful I can experience Your peace in the midst of my trouble. Amen.

Running With God

"Trust in the Lord with all your heart, and do not rely on your own understanding; think about Him in all your ways, and He will guide you on the right paths." Proverbs 3:5-6

I love running! Some people love golf, hunting or fishing, and that's great, but I love to run. It hasn't always been that way; I used to think of running as work. As a high school athlete, I associated running with conditioning or punishment. That perception didn't change much during my military basic training. We ran everywhere: to meals, to the rifle range, and we even ran to the track so we could run some more. Somewhere in the process of all this running, I began to change. Running became a habit, and it changed from work to pleasure. It became something I not only enjoyed but needed. During my daily runs, the world slowed down a little, and there were no interruptions. As I got older, the joy of running continued to evolve. The opportunity for some "me time" began to shift to an opportunity for some "we time." I discovered that my runs were the perfect opportunity to spend some quality time with God. I could reflect on the events of the day, and better yet, talk with God. God has been and continues to be the best running partner I've ever had.

Too often as runners, and in our everyday lives, we try to do it alone. We create our training schedules and decide we know what's best for us. This is a big mistake! We need to find ways to slow things down and get away from the distractions. We need to allow God to come alongside us and trust Him for direction in our lives. The truth is that we aren't capable of guiding ourselves. Trying to do anything without God's help is a recipe for disaster. A solo runner can get lost on an unfamiliar trail, encounter aggressive animals, or be left hurt and alone with an injury. Smart runners don't run by themselves, and smart people don't run without God. He knows us, He loves us, and He knows what is best for us. Keep running!

Heavenly Father, thank You for always being available to me. Take away my desire to run alone and teach me to lean on You for direction in my life. Amen.

How Will They Know?

"Now these three remain: faith, hope and love. But the greatest of these is love." 1 Corinthians 13:13

We needed an identity. As the head coach of a new high school football program, this was only one of the many challenges to be addressed. Sure, uniforms and equipment had to be ordered, potential athletes had to be identified, and a weight training program had to be implemented, but one other important question had to be answered. How would others know who we were? With that in mind, my next-door neighbor Dan and I began developing a new helmet logo. I had some ideas in my head, and Dan had experience as a graphic artist. What we came up with was a unique design that incorporated the first letter of the school name and a panther claw, which represented the school mascot. As we began our first season of competition, we would be known by the distinctive logo displayed proudly on our helmets.

As followers of Jesus Christ, we too have an identity. It's not the fish symbol on the back of our car, and it's not the cross around our neck. These things may help us look like believers, but Jesus wants much more. He doesn't want our identity to be defined by what we wear or display on our vehicles. To successfully let others know who we are in Christ, we have to go deeper. Peter Scholtes wrote the lyrics to a familiar song that explains what is expected of us as Christians. He wrote these words, *"They will know we are Christians by our love."* Symbols and logos come and go, but love never ends. That powerful message shared over two thousand years ago is still vibrant and strong in the hearts of Christ followers today.

Heavenly Father, teach me to put my identity in You. Help me grow deeper in Your love each day. May everyone I meet today know that I am a Christian by my love. Amen.

Perfection

"She (Mary) will give birth to a son, and you are to name Him Jesus, because He will save His people from their sins." Matthew 1:21

Everything was perfect in my eight-year-old world. Christmas was only a few days away, and I was excited. Our home-grown tree was up and decorated, the smells from the kitchen told me Mom was busy baking and I could almost taste the sugar cookies and cheese biscuits. It was beginning to look a lot like Christmas. Santa knew that at the top of my wish list was a football uniform. When the big day arrived, I was not disappointed. The uniform was there, and I couldn't wait to try it on. Quicker than you could say "Johnny Unitas," I was dressed with helmet in hand. I burst out the door, slipped on my helmet and fastened the chinstrap. However, something didn't feel quite right! I made a few adjustments with no real improvement. When I took off the helmet this time, I realized it was slightly warped. My heart sank with the realization that Santa must have left it a little too close to the fireplace when he took it from his bag. My disappointment quickly faded, however, when I convinced myself that playing football was more important than the warped helmet. Perfection is a good goal, but it's not a requirement.

Throughout history, man has sought perfection and failed. Every day, we wear ourselves out trying to be perfect on our terms and in our strength. We need to remember, however, that while God created us, He did not make us perfect. Thankfully though, that's not the end of the story. Through His grace and mercy, God gives us hope. That hope is found in the birth, death, and resurrection of His Son, Jesus Christ. When God came to earth as a baby, He told us we don't have to be perfect. He also told us we couldn't earn His love; it's a gift we can freely receive at any time. When we surrender to Him, a miracle happens! As the Holy Spirit works in and through us, though not perfect, we can be more than we ever imagined and God can be glorified.

Heavenly Father, may I never forget that Your love came in the form of a baby. That child, Your Son Jesus, is my only hope. Help me to accept Your gift and to share it with others. Amen.

Good Teaching

"...for I am giving you good instruction. Don't abandon my teaching."
Proverbs 4:2

"They're finally beginning to believe in the system we're teaching!" It's not unusual to hear a coach make this statement after a few weeks of practice with a new team. These words could come from a newly installed head coach or an assistant who's taking on a different area of responsibility. Whatever the situation, coaches usually bring their system and coaching style to the job. Players have to listen to what their coach is saying and adjust their style of play to fit the coach's instruction. Initially, it can be difficult for players, because they have the old system and the new system in their heads at the same time. With time and practice, the coach's new teaching takes hold and becomes second nature to the team.

Like a wise coach, King Solomon is passing along the teachings of his father to his children. The principles are proven, and Solomon is encouraging his children to do everything they can to live by these proven truths. He wants his children to see his father's wisdom as a family treasure. The Book of Proverbs teaches us it's wise to develop friendships with godly people with experience. Today, we would refer to these men and women as mentors. We can learn a great deal from their wisdom and benefit from their years of experience. As I reflect on my journey, I am thankful for the mentors who have shared their teachings with me. I am grateful God brought them into my life. Their wisdom has made me a better coach and drawn me closer to God. Their teachings have become second nature to me as I strive to live for the Heavenly Father. Good teaching–let's pass it on!

Thank you Lord for the wise people You have placed in my life. Thank You for their willingness to share Your timeless teachings with others. Teach me Father to see the wisdom in passing it on to those in my care. Amen.

Do the Right Thing

"...take up the full armor of God, so that you may be able to resist in the evil day, and having prepared everything, to take your stand." Ephesians 6:13

It was a pressure-packed contest with neither team willing to give an inch. Every ball was contested, and it was obvious the match would be decided by an unpredictable bounce. Then it happened! The ball shot from the mass of bodies, and suddenly it was a one-on-one duel between the streaking forward and a very anxious keeper defending the net. It seemed like I was watching a slow-motion movie. Frame by frame, I experienced a flood of emotions. When the ball left the forward's foot, I held my breath. My keeper laid out, and the ball sailed just wide of the right post. A deep breath of fresh air filled my lungs, and I knew we had dodged a bullet. As my keeper got up and brushed himself off, the referee signaled a goal kick and prepared for the restart. My keeper had a brief conversation with the referee and began walking slowly to the sideline. What's going on? Why was he coming to talk with me? He told me the referee had missed the call; the ball had gone in the net. There was a small hole on the side of the net, and on the bang-bang play, the ball had found it. The moment had come to make a decision; would I be thankful for my good fortune or would I do the right thing?

We never know how or when the enemy will come. In my personal experience, he usually shows up when we least expect it. Seldom do we have adequate time to think about how we will respond to his intrusions. Will we look the other way, will we call it a stroke of good fortune, or will we do the right thing? The Apostle Paul understood that when we take on Satan, we had better bring our A-game. When we put on the "full armor of God," we are prepared for whatever Satan can throw at us. We stand tall in His truth and righteousness, always ready to do the right thing.

Father, thank You for equipping me for my daily battles with Satan. Help me to make good decisions today and to always do the right thing. Amen.

Second Effort

"And if anyone forces you to go one mile, go with him two." Matthew 5:41

As coaches, we're constantly preaching the virtues of "second effort." In football, we want players to keep their feet moving, stretching for the extra yard. In basketball, we like to see athletes sacrificing their bodies as they hit the floor scrambling for a loose ball. In baseball, when a player races down the line and beats out an infield hit, we applaud his effort. Desire and willingness to give "second effort" can be the difference between winning and losing. It can also make an average player a great one.

Roman law required a person, when asked, to carry a Roman soldier's pack for one mile. All the soldier's equipment were in these packs, and they were quite heavy. At the end of one mile, the person could drop the pack and walk away. At that point, the soldier would have to carry the pack himself or find someone else to carry it the next mile. The law humiliated the Jews, yet Jesus told them to go not one mile with the pack but two! You have got to be kidding!

Jesus was telling the Jews, as well as each of us, not to just do the required. He is saying to go beyond what is expected, and do more good to others than is deserved. Why? Because we know that Jesus did far more for us than we deserved when He died on the cross. Too many of us want a "second helping," rather than a "second mile." We want to take the path of least resistance. Each time we encourage our players to give "second effort," we should also be asking ourselves if we are giving Jesus Christ the "second effort" He deserves.

Lord, thank You for the giving me Your best, even though I don't deserve it. Teach me to go the second mile in all I do. Give me the strength to never quit in my calling to serve You. Amen.

One Way to Play

"I am the way, the truth, and the life. No one comes to the Father except through Me." John 14:6

A common phrase used by coaches is, "It's my way or the highway!" This is usually interpreted as get with the program or move on; it's your choice. There can be one person in charge. Coaches want their athletes to believe in them. Coaches want their team to buy into the game plan, to trust that the right play has been called, and to be committed to executing the called play. Players must believe the coach knows how to get the best results. Teams that get on board with the head coach usually have a much greater chance for success.

In John 14:6, Jesus makes it very clear that He is the way to heaven. He is not one of many ways; He is the only way! Memorizing the Ten Commandments will not get us into heaven, and sitting in a church pew every Sunday will not do the job either. Deciding to be a good person also leaves us short of the mark. It is only through Jesus that we can come to God the Father. This means Jesus is the truth, not just someone teaching the truth. Truth can be found nowhere else. Jesus Christ is the source of life, and when we receive Him in our heart, we can have eternal life. Jesus is the way, but the choice to believe is ours to make.

Heavenly Father, thank You for providing a way to be on Your team. The choice is mine, and I choose Jesus. Amen.

Banners

"And Moses built an altar and named it, 'The Lord is My Banner.'" Exodus 17:15

Flying the banner of our favorite sports team is a long-standing tradition. A quick internet search will provide countless ways in which today's fan can display his or her team loyalties. We see banners hanging in our streets and from our homes. Flags, decals, and magnets of "my team" are standard equipment on every fan's car or truck. Team banners can be found in our game rooms and bedrooms, as well as on our mailboxes and front doors. We want the focus to be on our team, and we want everyone to know we stand side-by-side with them.

Over the centuries, God has been given many names. He is El Shaddai–"Lord God Almighty;" He is Jehovah-Raah–"Lord My Shepherd," and Jehovah Jireh–"Lord Will Provide." He is also called Jehovah-Nissi–"Lord is My Banner." Nissi is the Hebrew word for "banner." Following a great victory over the Amalekites, Moses recognized that Israel's success was the result of the Lord being their banner. As long as the focus was on God, victory was theirs. In battles throughout history, opposing countries have flown their flag on a pole. The purpose was to give their soldiers a feeling of hope and a point of focus. That is what God is to us–a banner of encouragement to give each of us hope and a focal point.

Lord, thank You for being my banner. In my daily battles, teach me to keep my focus on You. You are my only hope and salvation. Amen.

Never Quit!

"David said to Saul, 'Don't let anyone be discouraged by him; your servant will go fight this Philistine!'" 1 Samuel 17:32

How do you know you're defeated? When you quit! Ten years ago, the story of mountain-climber Aron Ralston made media headlines. While climbing alone in Utah's Canyonlands National Park, Ralston fell into a crevice and was pinned against the canyon wall by an 800-pound boulder. For five agonizing days, Ralston tried to lift and break the boulder without success. Seeing no other way of survival, Ralston decided to cut off the lower part of his arm using a dull utility knife. He then rappelled down a 65-foot wall and began hiking the eight miles to his vehicle. Following a chance meeting with a family of hikers, Ralston received food and water, and a rescue team was called. It was reported that it would have taken thirteen men, a winch, and a hydraulic jack to move the boulder and remove Ralston's arm. Under extreme conditions, Ralston refused to give up hope.

The story of David and Goliath is an Old Testament classic. For forty days, a nine-foot Philistine giant named Goliath challenged someone from the Israelite army to fight him. No one volunteered. It was then that the young shepherd boy, David, accepted the challenge. Despite the odds, there was no quit in David. He had developed great courage and fighting skills by protecting his sheep from the wild animals. After taking five stones from the creek bed, David stepped on the battlefield. He boldly proclaimed that he came in the name of God and God would be victorious. With one perfect shot from his sling, David killed Goliath. The rock didn't just hit Goliath; the Bible says, "The stone sank into his forehead!" After seeing their hero defeated, the Philistine army made a quick retreat. David did not give up; he stepped up! David knew, even in the face of incredible odds, that if God was on his side, there was hope.

Lord God, You are our hope in all circumstances. Teach us to focus on You rather than the giants we face on life's battlefield. May we boldly proclaim Your name and expect victory. Amen.

Adjustments

"Then He said to (them) all, 'If anyone wants to come with Me, he must deny himself, take up his cross daily, and follow Me. For whoever wants to save his life will lose it, but whoever loses his life because of Me will save it.'" Luke 9:23-24

In the world of athletics, coaches are constantly making adjustments. Football coaches move players closer to the line of scrimmage to slow down an opponent's strong running attack. Baseball coaches have their players move up in the batter's box when facing a pitcher with a good curve ball or off-speed pitch. Basketball coaches switch from man-to-man to a zone defense if they're facing a quicker team. Coaches unwilling to make adjustments usually aren't very successful.

Spiritual adjustments are important too! When God reveals His will for us, we must be willing to make the necessary adjustments to be obedient. We can't continue to live life as usual and go with God at the same time. Noah couldn't continue life as usual and build an ark; Moses couldn't stay in the desert herding sheep and stand in front of Pharaoh at the same time; David had to leave his sheep to become a king; Peter, Andrew, James, and John had to leave their fishing business in order to follow Jesus, and Saul (Paul) had to change directions in his life to preach the gospel to the Gentiles. To be a follower of Jesus, we too must be willing to make adjustments. Until we are ready to make those adjustments, we're of little use to God. Are you living for Him, or is it time to consider making a few adjustments?

Heavenly Father, we want to follow You, but we are weak and stubborn. Forgive us Lord and teach us to trust in Your promises. Help us make the adjustments that need to be made and use us today for Your glory. Amen.

Abandoned

"When it was noon, darkness came over the whole land until three in the afternoon. And at three Jesus cried out with a loud voice, 'Eloi, Eloi, lema sabachthani?' which is translated, 'My God, My God, why have You forsaken me?'" Mark 15:33-34

Have you ever experienced a time in your life when you felt abandoned and alone? I remember such a time in my own life when it seemed as though the walls were closing in. The situation left me feeling overwhelmed and helpless. I was frustrated with my job as a teacher and coach, my mother had been diagnosed with Alzheimer's, my Army Reserve unit was on-call to be activated and I was the father of two young sons who needed more of my time. The agony of the situation led me to cry out, "Where are you God, in my time of need?" My entire focus was on my mounting troubles, and I could see nothing good coming from the experience.

Jesus knows and understands our pain. Jesus was brought before Pilate for judgment and sentenced to death by crucifixion, given a crown of thorns, mocked, beaten and spit upon. He was taken to Golgotha and nailed on a cross with criminals. As Jesus hung on the cross, He was separated from God as He took on the full weight of our sins. In His final moments, Jesus cried out, "Father, why have you abandoned Me?" As Jesus took His last breath, I can only imagine the thoughts of the men and women who followed Him. Where would they go? What would happen next? When would the darkness end? Was there any good that could come out of this experience? What a difference three days can make! We know great things can and do come from bad experiences. We know that from the darkness of Good Friday comes the light of Easter morning and His Resurrection. God promises He will never leave us alone or abandon us, not even in darkest times of our lives.

Heavenly Father, thank You for always being there for us in our time of need. Give us Your strength to weather the storms and the dark times in our lives. Teach us to keep our focus on You and not our problems as we wait for Your perfect plan to unfold. Amen.

Gifted

"Now there are different gifts, but the same Spirit." 1 Corinthians 12:4

How often do we hear an athlete referred to as gifted? When that word is used to describe an athlete, we usually think of a star player like Drew Brees, Mike Trout or Kevin Durant. These men represent the best of the best in their respective sports of football, baseball and basketball. Each is able to play the game at its highest level and excel. The word gifted is defined as "being endowed with natural ability or talent." Nowhere in that definition does it mention that someone who is gifted is a star! Think about it—is the long snapper on a football team gifted? Is the pinch hitter on a baseball team gifted? What about the sixth man who comes off the bench to spark the starting five on the basketball court? None of these athletes would be called stars, but they certainly are gifted. Good long snappers, pinch hitters and sixth men are valuable commodities to their teams. Athletes with these gifts are needed to win championships.

I think the Apostle Paul would have made an excellent coach. He understood that everyone isn't gifted in the same way, but a variety of gifts is necessary to build a championship team. Paul wanted his team, the church, to be everything God called it to be. New Testament "stars" like Paul and Peter were pivotal in growing God's Kingdom. However, let's not forget the importance of role players like Andrew and Barnabas. They were not stars, but they were certainly gifted. Encouragers and those willing to bring others to hear the Good News of Jesus Christ are important in God's plan as well. What gift has God given you: great leadership skills, wisdom, compassion for young people, or simply wanting to make a positive difference in the lives of others? God is putting together a team of champions, and He is calling each of us to use the gifts we have been given.

Heavenly Father, thank You for the gifts You have given me. Teach me to use them in ways that will honor You and bless others. Amen.

It All Starts Here

"He said to them, 'Love the Lord your God with all your heart, with all your soul, and with all your mind. This is the greatest and most important commandment. The second is like it: Love your neighbor as yourself.'" Matthew 22:37-39

I don't know a single coach or athlete who doesn't want to win. Over the centuries, millions of words have been written on leadership, winning and success, yet the formula for winning remains elusive. "Work smarter, not harder," someone says. "Winners are willing to do what losers won't," says another. Locker rooms around the world are filled with slogans and quotes intended to inspire athletes with the will to win. What's the secret? Tom Chappell, American businessman said, "Never let the competition define you. Instead, you have to define yourself based on the point of view you care deeply about." In my experience, two things are critical in achieving success. One is passion, and the other is teamwork. Give me a group of individuals with a passion and a willingness to work together, and we can win!

The idea of playing with passion and as a team is nothing new. Jesus presented the idea when he was asked to answer this question, "Teacher, which commandment in the law is the greatest?" In the world of athletics, it would sound something like this, "Coach, what is the key to winning?" Scripture says that we must love God with every fiber of our being. That kind of commitment requires passion all day, every day. Jesus wants us to be all in! He wants us to "bring it" every play! But there's more; Jesus says there's another piece to the puzzle of winning in this life. We've got to love others as much as we love ourselves. He knew that "we" is more important than "me"! Jesus knew winning is much more meaningful when we have the opportunity share it with others. He understood the value and the joy that comes from playing as a team. No magic formula, no great mystery, winning requires passion and teamwork.

Heavenly Father, thank You for Your Living Word. Fill me with a passion to serve You in everything I do. Teach me the value of sharing life with others as I strive to be a winner in Your eyes. Amen.

Stacking W's

"Commit your activities to the Lord and your plans will be achieved."
Proverbs 16:3

Stacking W's! That's the phrase former Army football coach, Rich Ellerson, used to encourage the West Point cadets on his team. Coach Ellerson took over the Black Knights in 2009 and dedicated himself to reviving the historic program. To say coaching football at a service academy is challenging would be an understatement. Playing football is only a small part of the cadet's day. Juggling the academic and military training can be overwhelming, both mentally and physically. Coach Ellerson encouraged his players to not only accept the challenge but also to embrace it. By "stacking W's," Ellerson wanted his players to perform all their activities with a winning attitude. He pushed them to win in the barracks, win on the parade field, and win during summer missions—to be a cadet in everything they did. Ellerson said, "Winning is a habit and you've got to do it all day; you can't just flip a switch on Saturday." Good advice from a wise man.

What about "stacking W's" in our faith? What would that look like? When asked how we prioritize our lives, we usually respond by listing faith, family, career, health and on down the line. That can be difficult. When we start putting our lives in categories and ranking importance, it gets messy. It doesn't take long for faith, career, family and health to come into conflict. One solution might be to commit them all to the Lord. Why not put God at the center of our family, our career, our health and every compartment of our life. Why would we want the God switch flipped only on Sunday? What about letting God shine in our life seven days a week, twenty-four hours a day? Why not have His power on all the time! Have you committed all your activities to God? What's keeping you from "stacking W's" with Jesus?

Lord, I want to commit more of my life to You. Show me the areas I need to change so I can be obedient to Your plans through the power of Your Holy Spirit. Amen.

Have Some Fun

"When Jesus saw it, He was indignant and said to them, 'Let the little children come to Me. Don't stop them, for the kingdom of God belongs to such as these.'" Mark 10:14b

Practice was not going well. My high school soccer team looked awful! It had been a long season, and the high hopes we had going into the year had been crushed by injuries and unforeseen distractions. As I watched the guys go through the motions, my blood pressure was rising. There was simply no enthusiasm or energy. I had coached long enough to know that even though their bodies were on the practice field, their minds were somewhere else. The more I pushed and raised my voice, the worse they performed. In frustration, I blew the whistle and called the team in to take a knee. It was obvious to everyone in the circle that nobody was having much fun. The situation called for a different approach. I divided the sixteen players into four teams of four and we headed for the tennis courts. We spent the next thirty minutes playing tennis with a soccer ball. As the players worked frantically to get the ball over the net using only their feet and heads, something amazing happened. Their attitudes changed. The sparkle in their eyes returned; there was renewed energy, and it was obvious from the shouts and laughter they were having fun!

The word joy appears over two hundred times in the Bible, so God must think it's pretty important, but the joy scripture talks about is very different from the shouts and laughter my team experienced during that unusual soccer practice. The joy the Bible describes is supernatural, and it comes from God through the Holy Spirit. Are you joyful? If we belong to Christ, then joy is God's will for us. Scripture says there is a time for everything. There is a time for teaching, and there is a time for working hard. Surely, there must also be a time for fun and laughter too.

Heavenly Father, remind me often of the reasons You called me to coach. Help me carry out my responsibilities in a way that will honor and glorify You. Fill me each day with the same joy I felt when I turned my life over to You. In Jesus' name, I pray. Amen.

Too Much Information

"Excessive speech is not appropriate on a fool's lips; how much worse are lies for a ruler." Proverbs 17:7

It seemed innocent enough. Two friends, who happened to be coaching opposing baseball teams, just talking on a beautiful afternoon. As we stood on the infield grass, we caught up on one another's lives. We talked about old times, family and other topics. After a few minutes, the subject turned to the upcoming spring football schedule for our high schools. Unknown to me, my school's head football coach, who also doubled as head baseball coach, was listening in. After wishing my friend good luck in the day's game, I headed toward the visitor's dugout. As my thoughts shifted to the pre-game warm-up, up walked my head coach. He let me know very quickly and emphatically that what we did at our high school was no one else's business. It seemed silly at the time, and I got a little angry. However, as I matured and took on the role of head coach myself, I saw the wisdom in his words. What seems like innocent talk can easily turn into way too much information.

In today's world, it's even harder. Facebook, Twitter, Snapchat and other forms of social media make our every move public knowledge. What seems like innocent chatter can quickly turn against us. Looking back on my days as a classroom teacher, the worst place for idle talk was the teacher's lounge. How easy it is for small talk to sway our opinions regarding others. King Solomon warns us about excessive speech and the waiting troubles it can lead to. It's a wise person who knows when to "zip up the lips."

Heavenly Father, thank You for the ability to verbally communicate with others. Give me the wisdom and discernment to recognize the difference between helpful and foolish talk. Keep me in Your perfect will. Amen.

Relentless

"But we are not those who draw back and are destroyed, but those who have faith and obtain life." Hebrews 10:39

He just wouldn't quit! I'm sure our opponent that night didn't spend much time preparing for my miniature nose guard. He stood 5-foot-7, and the roster listed him at 160 pounds, though that was more than a little generous. His motor never stopped running, and his favorite response to my coaching directives was, "Come on coach, I can do it!" As quickly as the ball was snapped, he was in the backfield creating havoc for the quarterback and headaches for the head-scratching coaches on the opposite sideline. I love players like that! They don't look like much getting off the bus, but they are relentless.

Walking daily in the Christian faith is not a journey for the weak or faint of heart. We, too, must be relentless. On Sundays, as we stand with fellow believers, we feel confident and determined. On Mondays, the world hits us in the mouth and we must decide whether to stand our ground or draw back. The only way to survive is to be relentless in our pursuit of our Heavenly Father. We must pray relentlessly, study His Word relentlessly and serve others relentlessly. Physical stature isn't that important; God just wants a big heart and a relentless attitude.

Lord, I may not have much, but when I give it all to You and refuse to quit, we can accomplish great things. Thank You for showing Your strength through my weakness. Make me relentless for You today in all I do. Amen.

Preparation

"Slaughter the Passover (lambs), consecrate yourselves, and make preparations for your brothers to carry out the word of the Lord through Moses." 2 Chronicles 35:6

I once heard a pastor say, "spectacular achievement is always preceded by unspectacular preparation." As I watched a group of high school athletes sweating through a demanding summer workout, this quote came to life. A quick glance around the weight room produced no cheering fans, no marching bands and no scoreboard. It was early in the morning and the place was rocking. Coaches were shouting instructions and players were encouraging teammates. With precision the players moved from station to station, grinding out one repetition after another. Bench press, push-ups and curls, each being executed with perfect technique. The atmosphere was electric, yet outside the walls of that small room, no one knew what was taking place. What I saw was a team preparing for the upcoming season. I was witnessing a team being built!

In athletics, success is the by-product of preparation. The world seldom sees the endless hours of preparation that go into a victory on the PGA Tour or a Major League batting title. Success does not just happen; it's always the result of hard work outside the spotlight. Preparation is also important as we strive to live out a life of faith. Life is hard. We are either coming out of a tough time, going through one or anticipating one around the next corner. Are we preparing ourselves to stand strong when the hard times come? Are we building our spiritual muscles when no one's looking, so we can glorify God when they are? Are we studying and memorizing scripture? Are we on our knees daily in prayer? Do we have a good accountability partner? It's too late to prepare when the lights come on and the stadium is full. Success is something we all want, but few are willing to pay the price to achieve it.

Lord, thank You for not making it easy. As we serve You today, I pray for the strength to prepare and the wisdom to leave the results to You. Amen.

Win the Next Snap

"This is the day the Lord has made; let us rejoice and be glad in it." Psalms 118:24

The game of football has changed over the years. The smash-mouth, grind it out style has been replaced by hurry-up, spread offenses, designed to run as many plays as possible as quickly as possible. It's not unusual for these high-powered offenses to run 90 to 100 plays in a regulation game. The fast pace keeps fans on their feet and the scoreboard operator very busy. As exciting as running 100 plays in a game may be for coaches, players, and fans, the outcome usually comes down to one simple thing–winning the next snap! Plays have to be run one at a time, and if athletes and coaches spend too much time thinking about the next one, the odds are pretty good they're going to mess up the present one. Each play builds on itself. The more positive plays that can be strung together, the greater the chance of success.

This can happen to us in life too. Some coaches have their entire lives mapped out. They're going to work their way up the coaching ladder and take the head job at their dream school. They're going to get married and have three perfect children. After thirty years in the system, they will retire and live on the lake fishing every day. There is certainly nothing wrong with making plans for the future, but sometimes we forget that the choices we make each day determine the future we will have. Sometimes we're so focused on tomorrow, we fail to utilize and value each day God gives us. He has given us today, but there are no promises about our tomorrows. We must learn to rejoice and be glad in all that today brings. Tomorrow will come soon enough.

Heavenly Father, You made me and You have a plan for my life. Teach me to give You my very best each and every day. Help me to rejoice in today and not obsess over what tomorrow may hold. Amen.

Just Do It!

"Devote yourselves to prayer, stay alert in it with thanksgiving." Colossians 4:2

Nike's "Just Do It" slogan will be remembered as one of the greatest taglines in advertising history. The slogan cut across every demographic line and attracted attention in ways company leaders never imagined. It was simple, concise and easy to remember. It was a universal slogan that didn't connect with a specific sport or product. "Just Do It" was open to interpretation, and people adapted it to fit their situation. The slogan was not limited to sports and fitness; it was often connected to personal goals, like starting a business, proposing marriage or getting out of a bad relationship. As a result of the slogan's effectiveness, the Nike brand reached new heights.

The Apostle Paul never grew weary of coaching us on the merits of being diligent in our prayer-life. I've heard it said that one of our biggest regrets upon reaching heaven would be that we did not spend more time in prayer. Only then will we realize the extent to which our prayers were answered. There is a great deal of mystery, and an element of the unknown, connected with prayer. How do we do it? How long do we do it? What are the right words to say? Rather than spending countless time and energy trying to answer those questions, we probably are best served by remembering the Nike slogan, "Just Do It!" We are called to pray with sincerity, persistence and thanksgiving. God will take care of the rest. His love wants the best for us, His wisdom knows the best for us, and His power gets the best for us.

Heavenly Father, thank You for hearing our prayers. Teach us Father not to worry needlessly over how to talk with You but to just do it. May we be relentless in our efforts and always thankful with the results. Amen.

Perspective

"So if you have been raised with the Messiah, seek what is above, where the Messiah is, seated at the right hand of God. Set your minds on what is above, not on what is on the earth." Colossians 3:1-2

It was a typical conversation between two coaches. Following a very one-sided football scrimmage, one coach asked the other, "Are we that good, or are they that bad?" I had to laugh when I saw them look at each another and answer at the same time, "It's probably a little of both!" In athletics and life, we walk a slippery slope. When things are going well, we usually give ourselves too much credit, and when they are going bad, we take too much of the blame. Keeping the proper perspective in our lives can be very difficult.

The Apostle Paul addresses our battle with perspective in Colossians. As followers of Jesus Christ, how do we develop a heavenly perspective while continuing to live in this crazy, mixed-up world? We have taken the faith plunge and are learning a new way of life and thinking. But guess what; it's hard to live with your feet and head in different places. A.T. Robinson put it this way, "The Christian is seeking heaven and thinking heaven. His feet are on the earth, but his head is with the stars. He is living like a citizen of heaven here on earth." Jesus says there is a much bigger game taking place than the one we see on earth. This is not a task for the weak at heart; it takes hard work and discipline. We do it one day at a time. We keep looking up and striving to stay focused on the heavenly perspective.

Lord Jesus, teach me to see through Your eyes. Give me a heavenly perspective and help me live it out each day. Amen.

Hype

"But be doers of the word and not hearers only, deceiving yourselves." James 1:22

In the world of sport, thinking too highly of yourself is a dangerous road to travel. It's an easy trap for athletes and teams to fall into. The media and fans often go over the top in their efforts to build up a particular game, player or team. How often do we hear phrases like, "This will be the game of the century," "He's the best to ever play the game," or "They're the best team of all time?" We would agree that this kind of billing is hard to live up to, and flops in the world of sport are common. Coaches spend a great deal of time warning their players to be careful in reading their press clippings or paying too much attention to social media. Coaches too can get caught up in the hype. We can hear something so much that we start to believe it ourselves and forget to put in the work required to be successful. It's so easy to deceive ourselves, and the consequences aren't pretty.

James, the half-brother of Jesus, does not sugarcoat the issue. He is talking about the same principle but with much higher stakes. James believed the Scriptures could save us. He saw the Bible as an instrument of God that could not only help us gain eternal life but also save us a great deal of grief in this life. Like the wise coach, James warns that it's not enough to simply hear the words of Scripture, we must obey them and live them out. We must be willing to put in the hard work so that the word becomes flesh in our lives. Someone once said, "Impression without expression leads to depression." Bottom line, it's not about what others say or what you know; it's about putting in the work.

Father God, thank You for Your holy Word. Help us to take it from our ears to our hearts so we can live it out each day. Deliver us from the hype of this world. Amen.

How Do I Pray?

"You ask and don't receive because you ask wrongly, so that you may spend it on your desires for pleasure." James 4:3

It was a big game, and as his team took the field, I asked the coach if there was anything I could do for him. His answer was quick and to the point; "PRAY!" As we headed for the sideline to get ready for the opening kickoff, I assured him I would not only pray but would also pray without ceasing. That sounded like a great answer at the time, but as I stood on the sideline waiting for the opening kickoff, I was unsure how to even begin. Exactly what kind of prayers should I pray? In my selfish heart, I wanted his team to win, but does God care which team wins? Just because I know the players on my sideline by their first names, does that make it right for me to lift up selfish prayers? Doesn't God love and care about the team on the other side of the field too? Aren't they praying as well?

Prayer can be simple and complex at the same time. Anytime we need a good dose of honesty, we can count on James to give it to us. He tells us "you don't have because you don't ask." That sounds easy enough, so we pray "God give us a win" and wait for Him to deliver. But if we read on, we discover James wasn't finished. He goes on to tell us that God doesn't deliver when we ask selfishly or for our pleasure. In other words, God knows our heart when we pray. God sees a much bigger picture. There are many other ways to win than simply on the scoreboard. It was then that I prayed for all the players and coaches. I prayed God would keep them safe from injury. I thanked God for the gifts and talents He had given them to play and coach the game. Most important of all, I prayed God would be glorified in everything that took place on the field and the sidelines that night. Not only did God hear that prayer, but He also answered it.

Heavenly Father, thank You for hearing my prayers. Keep me humble and teach me to be selfless in my heart. Amen.

Motivation

"We love because He first loved us." 1 John 4:19

While sitting around the table with several golfing friends, the question was raised, "What motivates you to play the game?" The answers came quickly. One simply wanted to play better than he did the last time out. Another was very competitive and wanted to shoot the best score in his group. A third piped up that he just enjoyed being on the course and spending time with people he liked. Since I don't play golf, I felt obligated to tell my friends why I'm not motivated to play. We all laughed when I shared that golf was the only sport I've ever tried where the more I played, the worse I got! We agreed the game will humble even the best.

Let's use the same thought process and ask ourselves another question, "What motivates us to love God?" Some might say they serve God in order to get into heaven. Others may view God as a life insurance policy or a good luck charm. It's easy to serve God out of habit and not really think about why we do it. The Bible presents another idea altogether; it's called grace. Jesus, God's only Son, paid the price for our sin by dying a painful and humiliating death on the cross. This, and only this, makes it possible for us to enter heaven and spend eternity with God. We love God out of gratitude, even though we realize we can never give Him what He has given us. We obey Him, praise Him and serve Him because we want to. We love Him so much that we can't wait to tell others about His amazing love. We love Him because He loved us first.

Heavenly Father, thank You for loving us. Help us grasp the price that was paid for that love. Thank You for Your grace. Fill our heart with the desire to serve You and make You known to others. Amen.

Slumps

"Lord, how long will You continually forget me? How long will You hide Your face from me?" Psalm 13:1

As coaches, we have all watched helplessly as good athletes suddenly go into a funk and can't hit a baseball, make a foul shot or sink a putt. If that funk continues over an extended period, we call it a slump. Slumps are frustrating and can take a heavy toll on our present and future outlook. Slump victims will try anything in the attempt to get back on track. Baseball players often change bats, basketball players change the mechanics of their free throws, and golfers search for a new putting stance. Some athletes, in total desperation, resort to superstition like not shaving or getting their hair cut. Most are willing to do anything to snap out of a slump. Slumps can cause us to doubt our abilities and often create fear and frustration. The daily grind of battling a slump can drain us and isolate us from others.

If we are truthful, we have to admit there are times when we get into a spiritual slump. We're trying to do all the right things, but God seems to have gone on vacation. More times than not, spiritual slumps are the result of lost focus. The lost focus is ours, not God's. God hasn't abandoned us, nor has He lost His hearing. Instead, we've been too busy playing God and trying to do it all in our strength. Usually, after stepping back from our self-pity, we come to our senses and realize we haven't been trusting God. So what do we do to get back in the game? With an adjustment of attitude and a praise offering of gratitude, we can usually get back on track.

Heavenly Father, thank You for being a slump breaker and not a slump maker. Help me trust You completely, even when I don't understand my circumstances. Teach me to cling to Your promises, which You always keep. Amen.

Relentless

"But we are not those who back down and are destroyed, but those who have faith and obtain life." Hebrews 10:39

There is something special about athletes and teams who refuse to quit. What is it that motivates them and drives them to keep going despite the odds? What makes them so persistent in the pursuit of their goals? There's a powerful story of a high school football team in California, nineteen athletes and a coaching staff who are overcoming great challenges every day. This team is made up of players who share something in common; they are all deaf. As we listen to their stories, we feel their passion to be accepted and treated like anyone else. We cheer their persistence and celebrate their successes. We also see strength in what others might perceive as weakness. We see determined young men who refuse to back down and be destroyed. They are relentless!

Isn't that the approach we all should take? Doesn't living a life for Jesus Christ call for us to be unyielding and relentless in everything we do? We need to be reminded that fear does not come from God. As men and women of faith, we are called to move forward despite the challenges. We must remember that in Christ all things are possible. Like these amazing young men in California, we too are called to be relentless!

Heavenly Father, help me see the opportunities and not the obstacles today. Help me not to give up or back down from what You have called me to do today. Amen.

Character

"The one who lives with integrity lives securely, but whoever perverts his ways will be found out." Proverbs 10:9

My favorite coach of all time has to be John Wooden. His impact on the game of basketball, and those who played it, is legendary. Coach Wooden was once asked the question, "Do athletics build character?" His response is classic. "It can, and it can tear (character) down. It can do either one. It depends on the leadership." I believe that to be true. I say in athletics, given equal ability, the one with better character will emerge on top. By having character, you accept things better. You work harder. You don't worry so much about the other fellow. You do your best. I say let's have character, not be a character.

One of my favorite books in the Bible is Proverbs. The wisdom spoken in these verses is timeless and filled with common sense. Character and integrity are addressed clearly and leave no doubt in how followers of Jesus are to conduct themselves. When we live our lives with character and integrity, we will find safety and security. When we live a life built on dishonesty and deception, we will be found out and exposed. Our world has more than enough characters; what is sorely needed are more men and women of character.

Lord, keep me on the narrow path. Mold me into a person of character and integrity. Use me to influence others in the wisdom of Your ways. In Jesus name, I pray. Amen.

Adversity

"I will rejoice and be glad in Your faithful love because You have seen my affliction. You have known the troubles of my life" Psalm 31:7

"Why is this happening?" As coaches, we have asked ourselves this question many times. The pieces were in place for a great season, but it just didn't happen. You have poured yourself into the job for years, and now they want to fire you. We have a great season going; why are these parents giving me grief about their child's playing time? It's the biggest game of the season; why did my best player decide to get into trouble today? Years ago, someone shared this wisdom with me, and it stuck. "You can't run away from trouble; there's no place that far." Since it's impossible to outrun our problems, it's critical to decide how we're going to handle them.

Suggestions for dealing with adversity are abundant. "It will all work out in the end." "It isn't as bad as you think it is." And my wife's personal favorite, "This too shall pass." While each of these sayings holds a degree of truth, most of us want a little more assurance. Well, what does the Bible say? First, it tells us to put our trust in God. Second, it tells us when we pray to Him, He hears our prayers. Third, it tells us to move forward with faith and confidence in the future; God will not abandon us. God said from the cross on which His Son died, "I know the heartaches, the sorrows and the pains you feel, but I love you." God knows, God cares, and God will see us through.

Heavenly Father, thank You for Your unending love. Thank You for hearing my prayer and always being there for me. Teach me to trust You completely and to understand if You brought me to it, You will bring me through it. Amen.

Care

"I will instruct you and show you the way to go; with My eye on you, I will give counsel." Psalm 32:8

The most important profession in the world is parenting, and the second is teaching. As coaches, that statement should stop us in our tracks every time we see it. To me, coaching is teaching. When I look through the rearview mirror of my own experiences, without question, the most effective coaches were also the best teachers. While I've never played for a coach who didn't want to win, the best coaches wanted more for me. Not only did they want me to be the best athlete I could be, but they also wanted me to be the best person I could be. Because of what they taught, I became a better son, a better brother, a better father, a better husband, and a better citizen. Hall of Fame basketball coach John Wooden said this, "I wanted my players to know I truly cared about them. I loved them all. I didn't like them all, and some of them didn't like me all the time, but today I'm closer to many of my players than I was when they played for me."

God cares about us too. In His Word, God teaches us through wise instruction and counsel. He gives us the tools we need to make good decisions on whatever life may throw our way. Too often, however, we want to do it our way. Scripture says we are like the horse, restless to move ahead without command. Even worse, we are like the mule that refuses to go, even when directed. While God will always love us, He doesn't always approve of the decisions we make. When we aren't in tune with what God is teaching, He can and will discipline us to bring us back in line. Why? Because He cares. God sees a bigger picture. While we tend to focus on this life, God is preparing us to be citizens of heaven.

Father God, thank You for caring about me. Help me see the wisdom of Your teaching. Teach me to follow Your guidance and counsel. Help me accept Your discipline when I try to do it my own way. Amen.

Team Cohesion

"For as the body is one and has many parts, and all the parts of that body, though many, are one body –so also is Christ." 1 Corinthians 12:12

While talking with a group of coaches, someone made the statement that players today are better than ever but teams are not. Though I didn't want to admit it, I knew it was true. There are certainly some very skilled athletes I enjoy watching perform. Steph Curry, Mike Trout and Tom Brady are among the best at what they do. We also know that individual greatness does not always transfer to greatness as a team. Why is that? Well, sometimes great athletes are not great teammates. Larger than life egos and pure selfishness often get in the way of the team-building process. Every day we witness athletes consumed with personal greatness rather than team greatness. One of the biggest challenges for today's coach is how to successfully develop team cohesion. How do we take individuals with different skillsets and mold them into a team working toward a common goal?

The Apostle Paul struggled with the challenge of building a team too. Paul knew the members of his team had different gifts. He understood that if he could get them focused on a common goal, they could accomplish amazing things. Just like our modern day athletic teams, selfishness and egos got in the way. Paul used the illustration of the human body to drive his point home. The eye by itself is an eye. The arm by itself is an arm. The foot by itself is a foot. However, when each of these parts works together, they become the body. As a body, working together, wonderful things can be accomplished. Taking this a step further, as believers we are the Body of Christ. Whatever our differences, whatever our gifts, our common goal is to make Jesus Christ known to the world. We aren't asked to do this by ourselves. As a part of "Team Jesus," we can accomplish much more than an individual for Jesus ever imagined.

Thank You Lord for the gifts You have given me. May I use them for Your glory and not my own. Lord, help me to be a good teammate in the Body of Christ as we strive to make You known. Amen.

The Gift

"Do not neglect the gift that is in you...practice these things; be committed to them, so that your progress may be evident to all." 1 Timothy 4:14-15

Can you remember why you decided to become a coach? Many of us grew up playing the game and developed a passion for sports. It seemed only natural to move from being a player to being a coach. Coaching gives us the opportunity to remain a part of the games we love so much. As a young coach, I worked hard to earn the respect of my players and fellow coaches. However, I also selfishly enjoyed the status that goes along with being called Coach. Most of all, I liked the feeling that went with winning. As I matured, I began to realize there was so much more to coaching than status and winning. My entire outlook on coaching changed with the birth of my first son. It was then that I realized other parents love their children as much as I love mine. I began to realize my responsibilities to my players went much deeper than winning and losing. I began to understand coaching could be a ministry, and I could be a positive influence on the lives of others. I began to get to know my players; I listened to their concerns, gave them a voice on the playing field and treated them as I would have wanted a coach to treat my son. A funny thing happened along the way; I began to enjoy coaching more!

The Apostle Paul is reminding Timothy to use the gifts God has given him. He tells Timothy to practice them and be committed to them. The more we practice our coaching gifts, the more we will grow. The more committed we are to our gifts of coaching, the more we will understand that it is not about what we get. It's all about serving God with the gifts He has given us and positively impacting the lives of those we serve. It would be a good idea to ask ourselves occasionally why we coach. Is it for selfish reasons, or are we answering God's call to use the gifts He has given us?

Thank You Father for giving me the gift of coaching. Thank You for helping me understand that when I use that gift to serve You and others, You will bless me abundantly. Amen.

Extra Strength

"What does it matter? Just that in every way, whether out of false motives or true, Christ is proclaimed. And in this I rejoice. Yes, and I will rejoice because I know this will lead to my deliverance through your prayers and help from the Spirit of Jesus Christ." Philippians 1:18-19

At times everyone gets physically tired and mentally exhausted. It's interesting, however, that not all people react to this condition in the same way. Some stop and withdraw from everything, while others hit another gear and keep moving forward. It seems as if some people have extra strength. If I had a headache, I might take a Tylenol, but if I had a bad headache, I'm looking for the Tylenol with some extra strength! Now, some of you may be wondering where that extra strength comes from? For the record, Extra Strength Tylenol has more acetaminophen per tablet than regular strength Tylenol. That extra strength helps knock out your fever, aches and pains faster, so you can get on with your life. What about being physically tired and mentally exhausted; where can we find some extra strength for that?

The Apostle Paul says we can find an endless supply of extra strength from the Spirit of Jesus Christ. When we have given everything we have and our resources are drained, that's the moment Jesus Christ steps in. He has more strength and power to give than any of us could ever use. When we are weak, His strength lifts us up and gets us going again. If our hearts are open to Jesus, He can knock out all our spiritual fever, aches and pains. Do you need some relief? Just call on Jesus and the Holy Spirit.

Heavenly Father, thank You for always being there for me. Help me understand that You are all I need. Teach me to depend on Your strength and not my own. Amen.

Be Wise

"A fool's way is right in his own eyes, but whoever listens to council is wise."
Proverbs 12:15

I was in my first year of coaching, and I wanted to do things the right way. However, the junior varsity player was testing my patience. He was consistently late for practice, and I wasn't going to stand for it. I let him have it! I told him he wasn't fair to his teammates. I also said he wasn't committed as a player. This went on for about a week, but the situation wasn't getting any better. I was about to kick him off the team when one of his teammates pulled me aside and told me what was going on. He lived with his single mom, and she had to have the car to get to and from work. He was late to practice because his only means of transportation was to either walk or try his best to catch a ride. I was humbled and a little embarrassed. I had been so focused on my agenda and doing things my way that I hadn't bothered to get to the root of the problem or ask how I might help resolve it.

Proverbs 12:15 tells us you can't tell a fool anything. He knows it all, and he's not going to listen, but a wise man will welcome advice. He may even do something as amazing as ask for it. The wise man also recognizes it's impossible for one person to see all sides of a question or situation. Instead of making hasty or irrational decisions, the wise man will take the time to gather all the facts from all the possible sources. Simple concept, yet profound.

Heavenly Father, all wisdom comes from You. Teach me the ways of the wise and save me from my own foolishness. In Jesus name I pray. Amen.

Marriage

"Marriage must be respected by all, and the marriage bed kept undefiled, because God will judge immoral people and adulterers." Hebrews 13:4

As coaches, we have a lot on our minds. Our lives are a never-ending merry-go-round of duties and responsibilities. Everyone and everything seems to vie for our time and attention. We can easily feel as though we're living double lives as we attempt to balance career and family. It will come as no surprise that the biggest struggle facing coaches is the area of marriage and family. We often laugh and say we are married to whatever sport we coach. When a new season begins, we tell our spouse we'll see them when the season is over. I remember some challenging conversations with my wife as we discussed the strain of my coaching three sports and how to get the kids where they needed to be. Juggling a career we love with the spouse and family we love is difficult. Where are the answers to the tough questions we face in finding the proper balance?

Hearing what God has to say is a good place to start. The Bible says we are to honor marriage. Giving honor and respect to our marriage will take all the effort and conviction we can find. Society today continues to redefine the family, and the new definitions are often far from what God's Word teaches. God calls us to keep our marriage joyful and strong. We are to be faithful to our spouse in body and mind. We are to pray for our spouse, and we are even instructed to pray for the eventual spouses of our children. And finally, we are to model and teach our children the biblical meaning of marriage. None of this is easy, but God will guide us and He will honor our commitment.

Heavenly Father, make my marriage strong. Keep me faithful. Continue to teach me Your ways and protect me from the ways of this world. Amen.

Tenacious

"I am resolved to obey Your statutes to the very end." Psalm 119:112

"Just give me the ball!" You could see the tenacity in his eyes each time he took the mound. His illustrious career spanned 22 years, culminating in his selection to the Major League Baseball Hall of Fame. Greg Maddox was never overpowering at 6'0" and 170 pounds. He looked more like your college math professor than a professional baseball player. Put him on the bump and he morphed into a bulldog: strong, determined and not easily defeated. Maddox was the model of consistency–pitching more than 5,000 innings and winning 355 games, numbers that will be hard to duplicate. Once asked about pitching, even though his team was out of playoff contention, Maddox replied: "I don't care if we are out of it or not if I've got a chance to pitch, I want to." Give me a team full of athletes with that attitude, and we will win some games!

As followers of Jesus Christ, we too must be tenacious. The Christian walk is not for the weak of heart. It takes the same bulldog tenacity Greg Maddox demonstrated when he took the ball and walked to the mound for each of those 5,000 innings. There will be insults, hardships, troubles and even persecution as we walk the road less traveled. We must learn to hold on when times get hard; we must do all we can to resist the temptation to quit too soon. Our goal for each day and each lifetime should be to start well and end well. Good things take time, and we are usually rewarded for our effort and commitment. Greg Maddox is a Hall of Famer. When we hear those words, "well done, good and faithful servant," we'll know our reward is set not just for this lifetime but for eternity.

Heavenly Father, thank You for being a tenacious God. You never quit, You never give up and You can't be stopped. Teach me to put my complete trust in You and walk with You in faith. Amen.

What is a Coach?

"I will show you what someone is like who comes to Me, hears My words and acts on them:" Luke 6:47

What exactly is a coach? A mentor, teacher, tutor, instructor or trainer? An honest answer would be that we're a little of each of these things. Coaches wear a lot of hats and have unending responsibilities. Some say it wasn't until the late 1900s that the word coach was given an athletic meaning. The people who tutored Cambridge students in the art of rowing were called coaches. In the 16th century, however, the word coach was used to describe a horse-driven vehicle that would take important people from where they were to where they wanted to be. I like that definition because that's exactly what athletic coaches do. We take our athletes from where they are to where they want to be. They come to us with different personalities, skills and talent, but when they leave us we want them to be better athletes and better people.

Pride often convinces us we don't need a coach. We can get from where we are to where we want to be all by ourselves, thank you! As coaches, that trap can take us down some dark roads and off some slippery slopes. When we allow Jesus to be our coach and follow His teachings we are on a solid foundation. When the storms of life come, and they will, we can stand confident and strong. Trying to weather the storms in our strength is a recipe for disaster. With no foundation, our lives will collapse under the strain and be washed away. Where do you want to go? Let Jesus help you get there; He's the best coach there has ever been.

Lord Jesus, thank You for Your promises which give me comfort and peace. Remove my pride and teach me to depend on You. Coach me up and keep me on Your firm foundation. Amen.

Why?

"Let your good deeds shine out for all to see, so that everyone will praise your heavenly Father." Matthew 5:16

Taking inventory is something we often do as coaches. Typically when we think of taking inventory, we're talking about team equipment. How many basketballs need to be ordered for the season? Do new uniforms need to ordered and if so, how many? Taking inventory is a never-ending process for the coach who wants to be prepared. There's another inventory, however, that coaches often overlook. I think it's critical as coaches that we frequently take a personal inventory. We should ask ourselves three short questions and answer them honestly. *Why do I coach? Why do I coach the way I do?* And finally, *what is it like to be coached by me?* Coaches are great influencers, and they have the opportunity to change lives in both positive and negative ways. Keeping the answers to these questions in our minds and our hearts can help us maintain the proper perspective on why we do what we do.

Before becoming one of Jesus' disciples, Matthew worked as a tax collector, and tax collectors were not held in high regard in Matthew's day. No one likes paying taxes, but to make matters worse, the taxes Matthew was collecting were going to the despised Roman government. Matthew had a tough job, but his insight was important once he became part of Jesus' team. Like a coach, Matthew knew he held the power of influence. He could live a life that would draw others to Jesus or drive them away. He could speak the truth and be a light shining for others to see, or he could blend in with the crowd and ignore the needs of those around him. I think Matthew knew exactly why he was following Jesus. I also think he was trying his best to follow Christ's example. Most important of all, I think Matthew was willing to make changes in his approach when the situation called for it. What about you? Maybe the time is right to take your own personal inventory.

Heavenly Father, my desire is to glorify You in all that I do. Humble me and guide me as I take my personal inventory. Help me make changes if they need to be made. May others see Your son Jesus in me today. Amen.

Role Model

"But one has somewhere testified: What is man that you remember him, or the son of man, that you care for him? You made him lower than the angels for a short time; You crowned him with glory and honor and subjected everything under his feet." Titus 2:6-8

It's difficult losing a good friend. Bob was a gifted athlete; he lettered in basketball and baseball in high school and attended college on a basketball scholarship. After college, he served as a teacher and coach before moving into administration. For thirty years Bob was a high school principal, and he was inducted into the Hall of Fame by two schools. That's a great resume, but what I saw in Bob's life goes deeper than athletics or academics. Bob and his wife were married for almost fifty years and together raised two daughters. He got up and went to work every day with an attitude of joy and commitment, and he poured himself into the lives of others. Bob was committed to his church, loved his family and was one of those people that made you a better person just by being around him.

We all have influence, and each of us is a role model to someone. We may not want to admit it, we may not want to be and we may even feel that we're unworthy, but someone is looking up to us. In my times with Bob, the subject of sports seldom came up. Bob was always friendly and fun to be around; he never talked down to me or preached to me. It was obvious that Bob loved and cared about people, and when I was around him I knew he loved and cared about me. He lived his life, and others watched. Bob made a difference in people's lives. Do you ever think about where the next generation is picking up the lessons they need for life? Remember, everyone is a role model, but not everyone is a positive role model. You have a unique platform; remember that and, like Bob, change lives around you.

Heavenly Father, thank You for the positive role models You have placed in my life. Thank You for loving me so much that You sent your Son Jesus, to be the perfect example for living life. Teach me to love You with all I have and to love others as much as I love myself. Amen.

Baggage

"Aren't two sparrows sold for a penny? Yet not one of them falls to the ground without your Father's consent. But even the hairs of your head have all been counted. Don't be afraid therefore; you are worth more than many sparrows."
Matthew 10:29-31

Baggage. Every athlete we work with brings some of it with them. It doesn't matter what level we coach; we are responsible for young men and women with baggage in their lives. They come from homes and environments where the hurt is a part of life. Every one of them is looking for something, but they may not even know what it is themselves. The few hours of practice may be the only time they feel significant or receive a word of encouragement. For some, a coach may be the only person who makes them feel like they are worth anything at all. I wonder how many of us truly understand the critical role we play in the lives of our athletes. Sometimes we underestimate our importance. Not only can we teach them how to shoot a jump shot or lay down a bunt, but we can also teach them how to believe in themselves, be part of a team and how to bounce back from a tough loss. Each person, we coach, has value in God's eyes, so they should have value in our eyes too.

Jesus uses the insignificant sparrow to teach us an important lesson about our value. Not a single sparrow dies without God knowing about it. The same God who cares about a sparrow also knows how many hairs are on the head of each of His children. If God cares this much about sparrows and hair, just how much does He care about us and the athletes we coach? He cared enough for His Son to die on a cross so we can have the opportunity to live with Him for eternity. I challenge you to find the picture of the last team you coached. Look at the faces in that picture and realize God places a high value on each person there.

Heavenly Father, thank You for loving me, baggage and all. Help me see the baggage in the lives of those You have called me to serve. Give me the desire to pour into their lives as You pour into mine. Amen.

Who Are You?

"The evil spirit answered them, 'Jesus I know, and Paul I recognize–but who are you?'" Acts 19:15

Who are you? Think about that question for a moment. Do you know who you are? If someone were to ask you that question right now, what would you say? Would you tell them about your position as a coach at the local high school? Would you tell them about the amazing children who live in your house? Or, would you spend time talking about everything you're involved in at your church? Would you define yourself by your job, your possessions or your relationships? Too often our answers to the "Who are you" question reveal cases of mistaken identity. Coaching might be what we do, but it isn't who we are. Our family and friends might be who we associate with, but they don't hold the keys to eternal life. The only place in which we can find a true identity is in our status as a child of God.

Athletic and coaching careers end quickly from injury or age. We can lose our job in an instant. Our family and friends can walk away. But it's our position as a child of God that will never change. God is the only constant in our lives. If we aren't rooted in His eternal love and acceptance, we will eventually find out the hard way that all things in this life will fail and disappoint us. However, when we know the truth about a God who loves us with an everlasting and unconditional love, we will be free to live in the knowledge that we are eternally accepted; no matter what happens, we have a home in heaven with God.

Lord, thank You for loving me. Help me put my trust in You and not my job, people or possessions. Help me see that You are the only constant in my life. Amen.

Luck

"The plans of the diligent certainly lead to profit, but anyone who is reckless only becomes poor." Proverbs 21:5

In athletics, we're always talking about luck. How many of us have heard or said something after a hard-fought game like, "Luck wasn't on our side tonight; the breaks just didn't fall our way." I learned very early in my coaching career the lucky teams were usually the ones that worked the hardest. Sure, sometimes we face opponents that simply have more talent, but when evenly matched, the individual or team that has prepared themselves the best usually prevails. Lucky teams don't often win championships. Champions don't leave things to chance and good fortune. The formula for success is more often dependent on hard work than shortcuts or luck.

Hard work was valued in Solomon's day. To see a task to its completion was an accomplishment. In today's world we often get scared off by the idea of hard work, and if we do start something, quitting is often the answer when things get tough. Being a hard worker doesn't come naturally to most people; it's the result of strong character. Too often we look for a shortcut or the easy path. Usually, that approach leads to disappointment and a waste of precious time and energy. Solomon tells us to "work hard as if in the service of God." Surely we don't want to serve God with a haphazard or "whatever" approach. God gave His best through the life, death, and resurrection of His Son Jesus Christ. He deserves nothing less from each of us!

Heavenly Father, You leave nothing to chance. Lord, teach me the value of hard work. Help me give You my best every day. Help me also to give my best to those You have called me to serve. Amen.

Plans

"For I know the plans I have for you–(this is) the Lord's declaration–plans for (your) welfare, not for disaster, to give you a future and a hope." Jeremiah 29:11

Years ago I heard a newly appointed pastor announce to his congregation that he had a plan to make everybody happy. He went on to say many were happy he had come, and the others would be happy when he left. While we can get a good laugh from this, we know it's all too true–not only for pastors but also for coaches. Most coaches are planners. We create five-year plans to establish our program, we create game plans for each opponent, and we draw up plans for special plays in special situations. From my earliest days of coaching, I've heard that failing to plan is planning to fail. Well, what happens when our plans don't work out exactly like we thought they would? What if we're told we only have three years to implement a five-year plan? What if the fan base or the decision makers turn against us? What do we do when our plans don't work out and we are told that our services are no longer needed?

Despite all our planning, God is the only one who knows the future. Even though we think we're in control, we're not. The good news is that God's agenda is much better than anything we could ever hope for or imagine. I wonder what Noah was planning before God told him to build a boat. I bet Moses wasn't planning to bring the Ten Commandments down off the mountain when he was making the climb up. Surely, the Samaritan woman wasn't planning to meet Jesus when she went to get water from the well. I'm convinced God wants us to prepare and make plans, but I'm just as convinced He wants us to be open to His plans. What initially seems like a trainwreck could be the beginning of God's new and amazing plan created just for you.

Heavenly Father, help me see that my plans may not be Your plans. Teach me Lord, that great things can come from disappointment and hardship. Give me the strength to keep my eyes focused on You. Amen.

Holding Back

"For God has not given us a spirit of fearfulness, but one of power, love, and sound judgment." 2 Timothy 1:7

Too often in our lives, we're tempted to hold back. I remember when my oldest son wanted to play organized football for the first time. He liked the game and wanted to be with his friends, but he didn't possess what I would call a "football body." He was positioned in the secondary and loved to go for interceptions, but he was very hesitant of physical contact. As a result, I noticed he played much further from the line of scrimmage than he should have. As a coach, I knew this had to be corrected, but as a father, I had to tease him a little too. I told him he'd created a new football position. Instead of playing cornerback, he was playing "way back"! Just as I expected, he didn't see as much humor in the situation as I did. As the season played out though, he was able to overcome much of his fear and timidity. He learned a great deal about taking on new challenges and facing his fears with confidence.

There's a lesson for each of us in this story. The Apostle Paul knew about obstacles and hardship. He was imprisoned, shipwrecked and beaten, but he continued to move forward in God's call on his life. He refused to allow fear to control him. He neither held back nor did he put himself in the "way back" position. Paul knew that fear did not come from God. Being fearful and timid are natural emotions, but with God's help, they can be defeated. As a child of God, unlimited strength is ours for the asking. We may not always receive the outcome we desire, but we can face our fears with confidence and complete trust in our Lord and Savior Jesus Christ.

Heavenly Father, You are my strength in the difficult times. Teach me to put my trust in You and never hold back from the things You have called me to do. Amen.

Stress

"How long will you threaten a man? Will all of you attack as if he were a leaning wall or a tottering stone fence?" Psalm 62:3-6

Stress! We've all felt it. Sometimes it's self-imposed, and sometimes it's the result of everything going on around us. Every coach has dealt with it, is dealing with it now or will be dealing with it in the future. Stress affects coaches on all levels. It can make us irritable or defensive and cause even the strongest to question why we do what we do. If we aren't careful, stress can consume us and negatively impact our health. Some of us learn how to handle it, and some don't. Coaches are constantly under the microscope and our work is on full display for all to see. Media follows our every move, and internet chat rooms are filled with experts who know exactly what we could and should have done. How do we handle the stress? Where do we go for comfort and a little peace?

David knew about stress, and he wrote about it in Psalms. David was frustrated, and he let God know about it, but he didn't stop there. David reaffirmed his faith in God. That's a pretty good prescription for the illness. It helped David get what was bothering him off his chest, and it also helped him focus his attention on the one who could solve his problem. David didn't keep it inside and let it eat him alive! We don't have to be captives to stress either. It's a simple formula: pray, trust God and wait. It's difficult, but it works every time.

Father God, You are my comfort and peace. Thank You for hearing my frustrations. Thank You also for providing an answer to each difficult decision that must be made. Teach me to wait quietly and patiently. Amen.

24/7

"Go, therefore, and make disciples of all nations, baptizing them in the name of the Father and of the Son and of the Holy Spirit, teaching them to observe everything I have commanded you. And remember, I am with you always, to the end of the age." Matthew 28:19-20

I was coming home from school late one night and stopped for a Diet Coke and some much-needed caffeine. As I entered the store, I noticed a sign that read, "24/7," indicating that the business never closed! I could only laugh because as an Athletic Director, I knew the feeling. The A.D. is the person walking around with the most keys; they usually are the first to turn the lights on and the last to turn them off. A.D.s work alongside the school administration, manage their coaching staff and serve as the public relations expert in their community. Oh, and along with everything else, there's the mountain of paperwork that goes with the job. Paperwork related to eligibility, inventory and ordering new equipment, just to name a few. The price that goes with all those keys is the responsibility of always being there.

Too often in our Christian walk, we fail to understand what Jesus commands of us. Do we think of ourselves as being on call for Jesus 24/7? The Great Commission gives three commands. First, Christians are to go and make disciples; second, we're to baptize these new disciples in the name of the Father, Son, and Holy Spirit; and third, we're to teach them to obey the commandments of Christ. That can't be done on Sunday alone. It's a 24/7 process. It's possible Jesus has given you the key that will open heaven for someone you know. Are you willing to share the love of Christ with that person in the middle of the night, if that's what it takes? Jesus isn't asking you or me to do something He's not already doing. He tells us we're not alone in our task; wherever we go and whatever we do, He is with us.

Thank You Father for Your constant presence in my life. Teach me Lord that You are a 24/7 God. Give me Your strength as I strive to fulfill Your Great Commission each day. Amen.

Digging Deeper

"Like newborn infants, desire the unadulterated spiritual milk, so that you may grow by it in (your) salvation." 1 Peter 2:2

I was waiting, but 11-year-olds don't do that very well. The delivery of the daily mail had suddenly become more important. As a young boy who loved baseball, I had decided to take my game to another level. The Houston Colt 45's, along with the New York Mets, were the new expansion teams in Major League Baseball's National League that year. Responding to an ad, I had boldly ordered an official Houston Colt 45's scorebook and was eager for it to arrive. Finally, that day came, and I was holding it in my hands. Now, not only could I watch a major league game on television, I could document every pitch and every play. I could go deeper into the game than ever before, and I could go back and relive it anytime I wanted. I knew and loved the game of baseball, but now I could enjoy the full experience.

With the passing years, sharing that memory brings me joy and excitement. Surprisingly, it also makes me think of my journey with Jesus. Like baseball, it's difficult for me to remember a time when Jesus wasn't part of my life. Through watching my parents, I knew a strong faith was important. Later, the time came for me to make my own decision about Jesus, and I prayed to make Him Lord and Savior of my life. When that decision was made, the journey didn't end; it was only the beginning. I discovered it isn't enough just to know who Jesus is. I wanted to go deeper. I wanted to grow and be able to enjoy the full experience of knowing Him. Milk wasn't enough; I needed some meat! I found that meat in God's Word. Once I had a taste, I wanted more. With each bite, I grew and matured in my faith. With that maturity came another benefit. Not only could I go deeper, but I could also go back for another helping anytime I wanted.

Heavenly Father, You know exactly what I need and You always make it available. Thank You for Your Word. Teach me to go deep as I strive to grow in Your love. Amen.

Walking or Talking

"What good is it, my brothers, if someone says he has faith, but does not have works? Can his faith save him?" James 2:14

"Talk is cheap!" "Actions speak louder than words!" "He talks the talk, but doesn't walk the walk!" How many times have we heard these phrases or experienced them coming from our mouth? In today's society, we often say one thing but do another. Just tuning in to sports talk radio or television will tell us that. As coaches, we talk a lot. The words we speak are important because they can have a huge impact on those who are hearing them. Important as our words are, what we do is even more critical. The hard truth is that we will be known and remembered not only by our words but also through our actions.

James, the brother of Jesus, challenges us in James 2:14 to take a hard look at ourselves. How often do we tell the world who we are and then allow our actions to betray us? In his book, *The Mentor Leader,* Tony Dungy says, "one of the things that will define us is our faith." Dungy states, "Everyone believes in something, but the question we must answer is how passionately do we believe it?" Too often our faith is demonstrated through our words with very little conviction and even less follow through. This is a shallow faith unfit for others to follow. James' words are strong. He tells us true faith transforms not only our speech but also our actions. God wants our faith to transform every aspect of our lives. He wants us to be more about "walking" than "talking."

Heavenly Father, Your words have the power to change lives. Teach me Lord not only to hear Your words but to transform them into good deeds. Amen.

Excellence

"Blessed be the God and Father of our Lord Jesus Christ. According to His great mercy, He has given us a new birth into living hope through the resurrection of Jesus Christ from the dead." 1 Peter 1:3

"In the fourth round of the 2014 NFL Draft, the New York Jets select the offensive lineman, Dakota Dozier." That one sentence fulfilled an unlikely dream for a young man and many others who have become accustomed to watching him accomplish the unexpected. Dakota played his high school football at a school not known as a football powerhouse. He was an All-State performer and became the first player from his school to participate in the prestigious Shrine Bowl in twenty years. Passed over by bigger colleges and universities, Dakota signed with Furman University in 2009. Not only did he play, but he also excelled. Dakota grew into a 6-foot-4, 313-pound offensive lineman who was a four-year starter, three-time All-Southern Conference selection, and two-time All American. Did I mention that Dakota also plays the cello? He was named Furman's 2014 Male Athlete of the Year and graduated with a degree in health sciences. Dakota's quest for excellence is deeply rooted in his faith in Jesus Christ.

Scott Shuford, Furman University football chaplain, says "Dakota is a strong warrior for Christ! Over the years, I have watched him mature into a man who consistently puts Christ and others before himself. He is always fighting to better himself on and off the field, and I know that however his journey pans out, he will be found walking hand in hand with the Father." Dakota would be the first to tell you that God is the source of all his accomplishments. When we turn our lives over to Jesus, He empowers us in our quest for excellence. He gives each of us the strength not to simply participate in life but to excel.

Heavenly Father, You are the Great Provider. All we have and all we need comes from You. Teach us each day to live for You. Help us to never settle for average; give us Your strength and the desire to strive for excellence. Amen.

Gear Up

"This is why you must take up the full armor of God, so that you may be able to resist in the evil day, and having prepared everything, to take your stand."
Ephesians 6:13

In sports, having the proper equipment is crucial. Too often when we watch youth sports, we see athletes using the wrong gear or using it incorrectly. Little leaguers use bats and gloves way too big. Young basketball players shoot balls twice the size they need at goals way too high. Outfitting participants properly for youth football is not a task for the faint of heart. When preparing young athletes for competition, combining the proper equipment with the proper instruction usually leads to greater success.

A young David saw his family fighting the Philistine army and knew he needed to act. David had prepared himself for this day through prayer and working in his father's fields. He'd faced many tough opponents, including lions and bears, but Goliath was an animal of a different proportion. Over nine feet tall, he was a man among men who'd never lost a battle. King Saul offered David his armor, but David knew immediately it wasn't the right fit. So, he grabbed the equipment best suited for him, a sling and five smooth stones, and Goliath went down! Proper preparation, proper equipment, and God's direct involvement got the job done! Are you playing with the right equipment in your life? Too often we try to fight our daily battles with the wrong equipment. We try to battle sin and temptation in our power or with some self-help formula, but in reality, God's equipment–His word, truth, faith, righteousness, peace, and salvation–are all we need to defeat anything life can throw at us. Get geared up!

Heavenly Father, thank You for the lesson of David and Goliath. Teach me that in Your hands, small things become mighty. Help me understand that in Your armor, the impossible is possible. Amen.

Going Deep

"Therefore, brothers, by the mercies of God, I urge you to present your bodies as a living sacrifice, holy and pleasing to God; this is your spiritual worship. Do not be conformed to this age, but be transformed by the renewing of your mind, so that you may discern what is the good, pleasing, and perfect will of God." Romans 12:1-2

I love baseball! As a child, I remember urging my Dad to hurry home from church every Sunday so I could watch Home Run Derby on television. Each week, two home run sluggers of that era were matched against each other in a home run hitting contest. In an empty stadium, players like Hank Aaron, Mickey Mantle, Eddie Matthews and Ernie Banks would take turns "going deep" off the soft tosses of a batting practice pitcher. Anything but a home run was an out, and it was exciting to watch my heroes swing for the fences. The Major League All-Star game has recaptured some of this drama, and each July we're mesmerized as today's stars hit mammoth shots deep into the bleachers and out of the stadium.

While we love to see our baseball heroes "go deep," too often, we fail to go deep in our walk with the Lord. We find excuses not to attend worship. We fail to tithe. We don't discipline ourselves to pray. We use bad language and spend more time thinking about ourselves than we do others. What the Apostle Paul is attempting to get us to understand is the concept of total commitment. Jesus Christ sacrificed himself on a cross for each one of us. He was all in. If he was willing to die for you and me, then the least we can do is live for him completely. We need to be all in too! Every day we should look more like Christ and less like the world. With every pitch, the Home Run Derby contestant was swinging for the fences and looking to go deep. Our challenge is to take an honest look at our commitment to Jesus Christ and ask ourselves, "Am I going deep?"

Heavenly Father, thank You for being a God who is willing to go deep for Your children. Help me understand the significance of Jesus' death on the cross. Give me the desire and strength to go deep for You every day. Amen.

Seasons

"Then God said, 'Let there be lights in the expanse of the sky to separate the day from the night. They will serve as signs for festivals and for days and years.'" Genesis 1:14

There is nothing quite like the beginning of a new season. For a football coach, it might be the smell of freshly cut grass as he prepares his team to take the field on the first day of fall practice. For a basketball coach, it may be the shrill of that first whistle letting his athletes know the off-season is history, and it's time to play for keeps. Every sport has its unique sounds and smells which remind us that it's time for a fresh start. The past is behind us, and the future lies at our feet. Our hopes are high, and our excitement is difficult to contain.

As coaches, our careers are measured in days and seasons. Each day brings opportunities to pour into the lives of our athletes. Each season we search for the perfect chemistry and team cohesiveness that will make our team successful. To the average fan, the success of a season is often determined by the number of wins and losses. To God, it will be measured by how we shepherd and lead our flock. When the lights come on this season, will we be ready? Will we be ready to prepare our athletes to excel on the field and in life? Will we be ready to help them become good citizens, good brothers, sisters, sons, and daughters, in addition to being good at their sport? Will we be there for them when they fail or need guidance? Will we give them hope for a season or a lifetime? When the lights come on and the new season begins, will we be difference makers?

Heavenly Father, I want to be a difference maker this season. Give me a renewed desire to pour into the lives of those athletes You have put in my charge. I can't do it in my own strength; I need You if it's going to get done. It's in Jesus name I pray. Amen.

Quitting

"For they were all trying to intimidate us, saying, 'They will become discouraged in the work, and it will never be finished.'" Nehemiah 6:9

As practice was about to begin, two coaches watched the players come out of the locker room and onto the field. One athlete caught their attention. He was half-dressed, mad at the world and grumbling about the practice ahead. Shaking his head, one coach looked at the other and said, "That boy sure has a lot of quit in him!" Coaches are always watching and observing. We want to know how our players will respond to pressure and uncertainty. Times have changed, and it seems that quitting is a lot easier than it used to be. As it becomes harder to get athletes to come out for our teams, it's also an ongoing challenge to keep them there.

We can learn a great deal about the refusal to quit from Nehemiah, as he built the Jewish temple in Jerusalem. Nehemiah overcame many obstacles during this huge construction project, and his focus was always on its completion in a timely fashion. There were those who wanted Nehemiah to fail, and they were determined to throw obstacles in his path. Nehemiah kept one thought center in his mind. "I am doing a great work," he says. "I have a great calling. God has committed a tremendous project to me, and if I leave, it will be threatened." Surely there were times Nehemiah was tempted to slow down, stop for a little while or even just quit. But each time he felt like quitting, he thought about why he started. What a great reminder this is for us. I have heard there are three kinds of people in the world: those who don't know what's happening, those who watch what's happening, and those who make things happen. Let's be a Nehemiah and make things happen!

Heavenly Father, thank You for never quitting on me. Help me take a page from Nehemiah's life, and teach me to stay focused on the great calling You have given me. Give me Your strength Lord, and make me a person who makes things happen. Amen.

Fan or Follower

"Then He said to (them) all, 'If anyone wants to come with Me, he must deny himself, take up his cross daily, and follow Me.'" Luke 9:23

I'm amazed at how sports have become ingrained in our everyday lives. We are never more than a few seconds away from the hot topics of the day. ESPN, team websites, blogs and around-the-clock sports talk keep us connected to the never-ending stream of information on teams, players and coaches. Fans want to be involved; they want to know everything going on with their favorite team or player. Fans can also be very passionate. The reality is that fans are just spectators. They want to be close enough to their favorite team or player to get all the benefits, but not so close that it requires any personal sacrifice. Individual players and teams don't have that luxury. They have to be committed to putting in the time and effort to get better each day and to be physically and mentally prepared for game day. They are personally invested in the game while the fan is limited to a cheerleading role; there's a big difference!

How easy it is for us to fall into the same trap in our relationship with Jesus. We have the symbol of the fish on our car bumper, we wear the cross around our neck, we never miss a Sunday at church, and we have memorized all the words to our favorite Christian songs. So, we must be a follower of Jesus. Just like the sports fan, we often confuse passion with commitment. How easy it is to use all the "church" words, wear the Christian symbols and put on the appearances of being a Christian, yet never fully commit to being a Jesus follower. How often do we want the benefits of being a Christian without making the personal sacrifice? How many times do we find ourselves standing on the sidelines cheering instead of getting into the game? Jesus is not interested in having fans and admirers; He is asking us to invest, to put in a little sweat-equity and get into the action.

Heavenly Father, thank You for being committed to me. May I never forget the price that was paid for my sin. Lord, give me the strength to be a committed follower and not simply a fan. Amen.

A Bigger Picture

"The righteousness of the blameless clears his path, but the wicked person will fall because of his wickedness." Proverbs 11:5

Do athletics build character? Many coaches laugh and say, "It must because I sure have a lot of characters on my team!" But let's get serious. As a coach, is building character an important part of your program? I've heard it said that athletics could both build character and tear it down. If that's the case, what makes the difference? I believe the difference is leadership. What does that kind of leadership look like? An example of the kind of leadership that produces character was demonstrated recently when a veteran football coach stood before his team following their victory in the state championship game. "I don't want this to be the main thing you do in your life; I want you to make something of your life. I don't want this to be your highlight and go downhill from here. If you can do this, you can do anything, if you just keep applying the same work habits, the same discipline and making the same choices."

The Bible contains many examples of men and women of great character. A thorough reading will produce an equal number of poor examples. So what makes the difference? I believe the difference is leadership. One question we must constantly ask ourselves is this, "Who are we following?" Following Jesus produces the kind of character that makes our travels in this life a little less hazardous. It doesn't mean our life will be easy, just that we will probably have better work habits, be more disciplined and more likely to make good life choices. For those who choose to be characters rather than have character, Scripture says life will be harder than it has to be. The life modeled by Jesus paints a bigger picture. Jesus doesn't want us to settle for an average life or one that's highlighted by one win or one glorious season. Jesus came to show us how to live an abundant life, a life filled with continuous blessings and opportunities to bless the lives of others.

Heavenly Father, thank You for the wisdom in Your Word. Teach me to see the bigger picture of life. Give me the courage to be a coach of character for those whom I influence each day. Amen.

Guidance

"Without guidance, people fall, but with many counselors there is deliverance."
Proverbs 11:14

I didn't notice it when I took the picture, but now it's the first thing I see. At a recent team football camp hosted by the Fellowship of Christian Athletes, two teams had just completed an intense and competitive seven on seven sessions. It was hot and humid, but tradition called for teams to gather and pray together before moving on to the next game. Two teams, different in many ways, but with one common goal: "to see the world impacted for Jesus Christ, through the influence of athletes and coaches." The person who captured my attention was the smallest guy on the field and the only one who wasn't an active part of the competition. Without even realizing it, these athletes and coaches were guiding this young boy toward Jesus. With his hand firmly placed on his dad's back, this little boy was also connecting with his Heavenly Father.

God's Word tells us that without proper guidance, trouble will be our constant companion. On the flip-side, there is safety in having good counselors who exercise sound judgment. As athletes and coaches, many eyes are directed our way. This poem from an unknown author says it well:

> "There's a wide-eyed little boy who believes you're always right; And his eyes are always opened, and he watches day and night. You are setting an example every day in what you do; For the little boy who's waiting to grow up to be like you."

Father God, thank You for Your guidance in my life. Help me remember the influence I have on others. Teach me to live out my life in such a way that others will know you. Amen.

Confidence

"Let us hold on to the confession of our hope without wavering, for He who promised is faithful. And let us be concerned about one another in order to promote love and good works, not staying away from our meetings, as some habitually do, but encouraging each other, and all the more as you see the day drawing near." Hebrews 10:23-25

Count me in when it comes to good sports movies. I realize Hollywood always takes a few liberties in their storytelling, but *When the Game Stands Tall* is worth seeing. The incredible win streak of California's De La Salle High School Spartans grew to 151 straight over a twelve year period. As Coach Bob Ladouceur built this powerhouse, he emphasized individual purpose and significance over winning. Players play for their teammates rather than personal glory, they encourage one another when the times get tough and they openly share their hearts in team meetings. But when the streak is broken, the team must decide if the sacrifice, commitment, and teamwork they have always trusted can be rebuilt, as the world seemingly falls apart around them. As the team gets back on track and resumes its winning ways, we are reminded that it was never about the streak; it was always about the team!

In his book, *3D Coach, Capturing the Heart Behind the Jersey,* Dr. Jeff Duke says, "as people trying to follow Jesus, it's easy to lose confidence because as we live our lives, we're always missing the mark." Where do we go for hope? Where do we go for encouragement? Scripture tells us to hold on and never waver! God's Word tells us He was faithful yesterday, and He will be faithful today. We're also reminded to take our eyes off of ourselves and put them on others. In our "me" society, that can be difficult to do. Lastly, we are challenged to love each other and encourage one another. As we go through life, we will have our winning streaks and our losing streaks. There will be times when we lose hope and don't know where to turn. The answer is always Jesus. He is always there, and He always has our back!

Lord, make me an encourager. Give me the wisdom to speak greatness into those whom I influence. Allow my words and my actions to change lives. Make me a living testimony to Your great love. Amen.

Do You Believe It?

"Immediately he began proclaiming Jesus in the synagogues: 'He is the Son of God.'" Acts 9:20

Early in my coaching career, I was given the opportunity to become head coach of a small high school that had never had a football program. We had nothing! No field, no equipment, no locker room, no weight room and no players. What we did have was a community that wanted a football program very badly and a young coach who was too naive to understand the enormity of the situation. I'll never forget a meeting with the players and their parents at the beginning of that first season. We had purchased new equipment for the team, and I wanted the parents to know their sons were well protected and safe. I had one of my players stand on a table in the cafeteria and proceeded to dress him from head to toe, one piece of equipment at a time. Truth be known, this was the first time most of the parents had ever seen shoulder pads and helmets up close. My job was to get these parents to believe their sons were well protected. If I didn't believe my athletes were safe, how could they believe it?

Saul's life was turned upside down on the road to Damascus. On his journey to persecute Christians, Saul became one himself. How could that be? In the local synagogues, Saul boldly proclaimed that Jesus is the Son of God. Those listening to Saul's words knew he had only recently hated the name of Jesus, and now he was teaching that Jesus was God. Many hearing Saul did not believe their ears. They did not trust him and even wanted to kill him, but this did not stop Saul. Scripture says he became "more capable." In other words, Saul believed in what he was saying and slowly others began to believe as well. We know the rest of the story as Saul became Paul, one of God's true warriors for the faith. What about your faith? What do you believe? How convincing are you in your words and actions?

Heavenly Father, take away my doubts today. Help me become more capable as I share Your promises with others. Use me today as one of Your warriors for the faith. Amen.

Hope

"For God so loved the world in this way: He gave His One and Only Son, so that everyone who believes in Him will not perish, but have eternal life. For God did not send His Son into the world that He might condemn the world, but that the world might be saved through Him." John 3:16-17

Sometimes as coaches, we find ourselves in a hopeless situation. Watching the final seconds tick off the clock and being on the wrong end of a 62-0 football beat down is one of those times. Trying to be positive as you prepare your vertically challenged basketball team to take on a team of giants does not inspire great optimism. Being fearful for the safety of your infielders as your best pitcher is being lit up by your opponent makes you want to stay in the dugout when the game is over. Hopelessness is defined as "having no possibility of a solution." We have all been there. One of the great things about sports is there is usually another game to play. As coaches, we continue to care about our players; we stand with them in the tough times, and we keep encouraging them. As a team, we confidently keep working to improve, with the hope that a new day will bring better results.

In our everyday lives, we also often find ourselves in seemingly hopeless situations. Illness, loss of a loved one, unemployment, bankruptcy and loneliness are just a few that come to mind. Where can we find hope in the hopelessness of life? God is the solution! John 3:16 is one of the best-known verses in the Bible. It tells us God loves us, and He always will. Love is just who God is! As the Master Coach, God will never abandon us. He is always with us, in the good times and the bad. Finally, God is for us. He is not out to get us or make us miserable. He is on our side, encouraging us to live our lives with purpose and meaning. Need some hope in your life today? Talk with God. He would love to hear from you.

Heavenly Father, You are our only hope. Teach us to give it all to You today. Thank for You for loving us more than we could ever imagine. Amen.

Walking Straight

"Teach me Your way, Lord, and I will live by Your truth. Give me an undivided mind to fear Your name." Psalm 86:11

If I had a dollar for every line I've painted on an athletic field, I'd be a wealthy man! Preparing a field for competition is an art, and it also requires having the right equipment. I learned early in my coaching career that the best way to line a field is to do it right the first time. By having the right tools, taking your time and staying focused, you can be proud of the finished product. Painting a straight line is not as easy as it might seem, and I would never attempt to paint any line without a reel of string on hand. By stretching the string from sideline to sideline, anyone with a steady hand and a keen eye can do a good job. However, if you try to go too fast or take your eyes off the string, your lines will snake in every direction. To anyone sitting in the stands, it's easy to tell if the person painting the lines was focused and walking straight.

As we look at our world today, a lot of crooked lines are being painted. One explanation for all these crooked lines is that too often we try to do things our way. We take shortcuts that wind up costing us time and generating frustration. We don't have the right tools on hand, or even worse, we don't bother to follow the instructions for doing the job. Too often, we fail to stretch the string across the field to help us walk a straight line to the other side. What a great reminder we have in Psalms about the importance of walking straight and upright before God. God and His Word are our string. When we walk according to His direction, He will give us what is good and multiply our blessings. When we walk following His string, our paths will be straight.

Heavenly Father, thank You for Your string. Give us the wisdom to stretch it out and apply it to every aspect of our lives. Teach us to walk the straight path with You. Amen.

Are You Discouraged?

"And if the Spirit of Him who raised Jesus from the dead lives in you, then He who raised Christ from the dead will also bring your mortal bodies to life through His Spirit who lives in you." Romans 8:11

As coaches, we are affected by unique pressures and stresses in our lives. Coaches are busy people! Thinking back on my early years in coaching, I remember teaching five classes each day, coaching a sport each afternoon and then going home to prepare lesson plans and practice schedules for the next day. There were papers to grade, film to study and games to play, on top of everything else. Throw in church activities, paying the bills, maintaining the yard and spending quality time with our children, and I wonder how my body held up and my marriage survived. Rest and sanity can be hard to find. There are many good things we desire to do but simply don't have the energy or time to do them. We are overloaded and maxed out. With these kinds of schedules, it's easy to get discouraged.

Discouragement is one of Satan's biggest weapons, and he is the master of knowing how and when to use it. His most successful attacks come when we are tired and weak. It is then that we are most likely to fall for his lies. He works on our emotions and tries to convince us we are accomplishing nothing of value. He hammers us with guilt and takes away our ability to think rationally. What can we do when these attacks come? Like a physically tired and stressed athlete goes for the energy drink, we need to reach for a taste of the Holy Spirit. Romans 8:11 offers encouragement and tells us that the Holy Spirit will bring our tired and stressed bodies back to life. We can be refreshed and rejuvenated with "new life." Because the Holy Spirit lives in us, there is never a time when we don't have everything we need.

Heavenly Father, sometimes the pressure and stress of life can overwhelm us. Teach us the value of rest. Help us understand You are all we need. Amen.

View from the Press Box

"For My thoughts are not your thoughts, and your ways are not My ways,' (This is) the Lord's declaration. 'For as heaven is higher than earth, so My ways are higher than your ways, and My thoughts than your thoughts.'" Isaiah 55:8-9

Sometimes we're too close to a situation to see what's really going on. Most coaches like being on the sidelines. Standing on the sidelines puts us close to the action and allows us to be involved in the natural flow of the game. It seems easier to interact with the players and coaches and make offensive and defensive adjustments. There are also negatives to being on the sidelines. Our view of the action can be limited and even distorted. Being too close to the action can limit our perspective. That's why we put coaches in the press box. The "eye in the sky" gives us a different viewpoint, and we get a much larger and more accurate picture of what's taking place. In the play-calling process, coaches on the sidelines trust the view from the press box.

Isaiah, the Hebrew prophet, tells us we're wise when we commit to a one-to-one relationship with God. Why? Because God has a much better perspective than we do. How often do we stubbornly try to call the plays for our life from the sidelines, trusting in our own limited and distorted viewpoint? Why is it so hard to let God call the plays from the press box? A. W. Tozer says, "God must do everything for us. Our part is to yield and trust." God is a jealous God; He knows us better than we know ourselves, and He wants us to focus on Him first. Our Heavenly Father will meet our every need. Will you put all your trust in Him today?

Lord, you are a jealous God and I know You want all of me, not part of me. Take away my doubt and my pride. Teach me to put my complete trust in You and Your Word. Amen.

Grinders

"Therefore, my dear brothers, be steadfast, immovable, always excelling in the Lord's work, knowing that your labor in the Lord is not in vain." 1 Corinthians 15:58

Coaches love grinders! A grinder is an athlete who succeeds through hard work and determination rather than exceptional talent or skill. Grinders show up every day, they are eager to work, and they place team before self. In my opinion, grinders become excellent coaches. Coaches from this mold seldom allow disappointment to turn into discouragement. They welcome each day as a chance to get better, individually and as a team. They understand what they are doing goes far beyond what the average fan sees on game day. Grinders believe the words of the great English writer Samuel Johnson, "Great works are not accomplished by strength but by perseverance." Hard work sustained over a period of time is usually rewarded.

God knows and comes alongside those who are committed to doing His will. We can find comfort in the fact that grinding for God is never in vain. We must not allow ourselves to get discouraged or give up. God wants us to keep showing up, ready to work and putting the needs of others first. He will take our service and use it for His purpose. He is always there giving us the strength to persevere when the times get tough and the troubles come. It's a new day—keep grinding!

Father, thank You for loving me. Teach me and equip me to be a grinder for You. May I never give up, give in or give out in my service to You. Amen.

Keep It Simple

"When you pray, don't babble like the idolaters, since they imagine they'll be heard for their many words." Matthew 6:7

As a junior varsity football coach, I quickly learned the importance of keeping things simple. One of my goals each season was to get the offense to execute five running plays and three passing plays with confidence and precision. However, the temptation to expand the play book was always in the back of my mind. How would it look to other coaches or fans if they knew I only had eight plays? Would they think I wasn't very smart or just a poor coach? Wouldn't it be more difficult for opposing coaches to prepare if we had sixteen plays or maybe twenty-four? What I came to realize was if my team could execute eight plays effectively, we had a chance against anyone. I learned it was more important to run a few plays well than it was to try and impress others with a big play book my players couldn't master.

Our prayer life can be like that if we aren't careful. How often do we hear repetitious prayers filled with emptiness? It could be a blessing before a meal or saying our prayers before going to bed at night. No real connection to God, just words. Sometimes we may even pray as though we are trying to impress God. We think the more words we use the more God will like it. If we use some big "church" words, it's even better. I believe God is more interested in our sincerity and our heart than He is about the number and size of our words. Former New York Yankee great, Bobby Richardson, was once asked to pray at an event and prayed these words, "Dear God, Your will, nothing more, nothing less, nothing else, Amen." I have no doubt God heard and appreciated that request. Remember, quality is more important to God than quantity.

Heavenly Father, thank You for loving me. Teach me to keep it simple as I strive to know You better today. Amen.

Transformed

"Therefore, brothers, by the mercies of God, I urge you to present your bodies as a living sacrifice, holy and pleasing to God; this is your spiritual worship. Do not be conformed to this age, but be transformed by the renewing of your mind, so that you may discern what is good, pleasing, and the perfect will of God." Romans 12:1-2

One of the joys of coaching is watching young players grow and mature. A skinny and awkward 15-year-old can come back from a summer vacation looking like a different person. It isn't unusual for an athlete this age to put on twenty pounds and grow several inches in a very short period. It's also possible for a young athlete to look completely lost and confused for much of the season, then have the light come on and compete like he has played all his life. These transformations are as beautiful in the eyes of a coach as watching a caterpillar become a butterfly is to a botanist.

In Romans 12:1-2, Paul speaks about the transformation that should take place in our lives when we accept God's grace. There should be a sharp contrast in the before and after. Paul says we must make a total commitment to God, and our lives are to be a living sacrifice to Him. British athlete C.T. Studd said, "If Jesus Christ is God and died for me, then no sacrifice can be too great for me to make for Him." We must pay attention to the music we listen to, the thoughts we have and the ever-present urge to conform to the world we live in. We must give Him not only our lives but our service, our praise, and our possessions. We must learn, as best we can, to think as God thinks. When we sacrifice our body, separate ourselves from the world and transform our mind, we can find God's perfect will for our life. That's a life worth living!

Heavenly Father, thank You for Your gift of grace. Teach me the full meaning of that gift and transform me today into a vessel that can be used for Your glory. Amen.

Joy

"I greatly rejoice in the Lord..." Isaiah 61:10a

I have experienced many joys during my years of coaching. Being part of a state championship football team, winning region titles and celebrating victories over major rivals are but a few of my joyful memories. Seeing great effort and hard work bear fruit has been a joy. I also remember the joy in getting notes from parents of athletes, thanking me for being a positive influence in the lives of their sons. It still brings me joy when I hear the words "Hey Coach" and get the chance to catch up on the life of a former athlete. Joy is all around us if we only take the time to look.

Joy is one of the major themes of the Bible. I understand there are 323 references to the concept of joy found in the Bible, so it must be a big deal to God! Joy is defined as "the feeling of great happiness or pleasure." Biblically, joy is defined as "the happy state that results from knowing and serving God." What a difference! Seldom does our pursuit of happiness and pleasure bring lasting joy or fulfillment. Too much pleasure can be bad for us, but we can never experience too much joy. God created joy! We will never experience a greater joy than turning our lives over to Him and walking with Him every minute of every day.

Heavenly Father, thank You for the joy You have placed in my life. Help me not only to see it clearly today but to give it away to others. Amen.

New Beginnings

"Therefore, if anyone is in Christ, there is a new creation; old things have passed away, and look, new things have come." 2 Corinthians 5:17

Every season brings new players, new chemistry, new goals and new experiences. No matter how long we've been coaching, there's something that stirs in us as new seasons approach. We have a chance to leave the previous season behind. Maybe we lost more games than we won, the team didn't gel like we thought it would, injuries crippled the team, or maybe we fell short of our preseason goals. That's in the past. We're excited about what the new season can bring and can't wait to get started!

In our scripture, Paul reminds us that when we give our lives to Christ, we can put our past behind us and live in a new way. We become a new creation and are no longer judged by the same standards. When Christ is in us, we begin to think less about how others see us and more about how God sees us. Our surrender to Christ allows us to be born again into a new life. We can bury the disappointments and failures of our past and start a new journey of obedience to our Lord and Savior. That too should excite us! If you haven't decided to follow Christ, what are you waiting for? If you have decided to follow Christ but aren't sharing the opportunity with those you love and care about, what's holding you back?

Thank You Father for being a God of new beginnings. As another day approaches, help me live it for You. Amen.

Family

"Unless the Lord builds the house, its builders labor in vain; unless the Lord watches over a city, the watchmen stays alert in vain." Psalm 127:1

Let's face it, being a coach at any level is hard on the family life. As coaches, we're pulled away from our homes and families a great deal. The profession requires us to study film, prepare practice schedules and speak to outside groups, in addition to trying to put a quality product on the field or court. We can find ourselves being criticized in the media, in chat rooms and even in the local barber shop or grocery store. Our spouses and children sit in the stands and hear the "Monday Morning Quarterbacks" shout out what they would have done in a key situation. With all these things going on, it can be difficult for a coach to keep his or her priorities right and maintain a normal life. Mark Richt, head football coach of the Miami Hurricanes, puts a high priority on family. His morning staff meetings are late enough that his assistants can help get their kids to school. He plans a family night, so coaches can bring their wives and children to have dinner with the players. He schedules lunches with his wife, eats lunch at school with his kids and has dinner with his family in the evening. Coach Richt is a leader of men, teaching his players loyalty, integrity, hard work, and honesty. He is also teaching them that real men take care of their families.

There is a saying "Little is much if God is in it," but the opposite is also true. Much is nothing if God is not in it. Psalm 127:1 reminds us that unless our coaching is directed by the Lord, it is a waste of time and energy. We can have great teams and put up impressive statistics, but unless we put God in it, most of what we do is worthless. The coach who lives by God's standards, enjoys the relationship with their spouse and is proud of their children, is richly blessed.

Heavenly Father, thank You for the gift of family. Today, give me the wisdom and strength to put You in the middle of the relationships I have with my spouse and children. Help me focus on the things that will last for eternity. Amen.

Team Meeting

"Woe to you experts in the law! You have taken away the key to knowledge! You didn't go in yourselves, and you hindered those who were going in." Luke 11:52

We all know about the team meeting. When things aren't going well, the coach gathers his/her players together in the locker room for a one-sided discussion on what they have been doing wrong. I don't know anyone who enjoys these sessions, and as coaches, we must be careful not to have them too often. When used properly, however, team meetings can help clear the air and shift the team's focus to things that are truly important. Jesus called a team meeting with the Pharisees after observing their inconsistent actions. He let them know their outward appearance didn't match their heart. Jesus told them they were morally corrupt and created a burden on the people with all their laws. How's that for a tongue lashing?

It's easy for our lives to mirror the Pharisees. If Jesus were to have a team meeting with you today, what would He talk about? Are your actions consistent with your talk? Are you honest with yourself and with God, or are you just trying to put up a good front? We need to search our heart daily. We need to find everything that doesn't belong there, confess it and ask God for forgiveness. Slowly, we can remove the junk that fills our heart and begin to focus on the things that are truly important.

Heavenly Father, help me to remove the junk from my life today. Replace it with things that matter for Your Kingdom and for eternity. Amen.

Xs And Os

"And what you have heard from me in the presence of many witnesses, commit to faithful men who will be able to teach others also." 2 Timothy 2:2

Who can't remember those childhood days when the neighborhood kids got together for a backyard game of football? We divided into teams, decided who would play what position and then began to make up our plays. Plays could be drawn up in the dirt, or the quarterback could simply tell his receiver to run down the field twenty yards and head for the trash can. As coaches, we are sometimes obsessed with the Xs and Os of the game. We go to clinics, read books and pick other coaches' brains to come up with plays that can make our team better. While the plays are important, so are the athletes we teach to execute those plays. Are we providing the spiritual strength our players need? Coaches have the opportunity to influence and change lives. Coaches can be the great multipliers! It's up to us to teach in such a way that will strengthen and encourage others to carry on as competent teachers when we are long gone.

The Apostle Paul knew his time was short, and he faithfully taught Timothy to carry on the ministry. Timothy was also responsible for preparing others to carry on as teachers of the gospel when his days were over. 2 Timothy 2:2 is telling us the importance of making disciples. As Christian coaches, we should teach the game, but we should also provide the spiritual strength our athletes need. We should strive to share the truths that will make them faithful men and women, who in turn will be able to teach others how to live for Jesus Christ. I have heard it said this way–"We can choose to be role models or parole models." Think about it!

Lord, help me today to live my life in such a way as to be a positive example to those You have called me to serve. Amen.

Dedication

"Therefore, all who are mature should think this way. And if you think differently about anything, God will reveal this to you also. In any case, we should live up to whatever (truth) we have attained. Join in imitating me, brothers, and observe those who live according to the example you have in us."
Philippians 3:15-17

There is nothing quite like game day! The scouting has been done, a game plan has been prepared and there is no more time to practice. Coaches and athletes are united; it's crunch time! It's time to put on the equipment, trust in what we have learned and get into action. Everyone has a role to play, and each person is focused on executing his role. Regardless of how prepared we are, games usually don't go as planned. Adversity comes, and we are faced with the decision of staying committed to what we are doing or going in another direction. Experience and maturity are needed to prevent panic. A hasty decision can determine the outcome of the game.

The Apostle Paul encouraged followers of Jesus to stay committed, and he urged Christians to be imitators of his walk. While this may seem rather bold, Paul's life following his conversion was a model of devotion to Jesus Christ. Paul was willing to suffer and die for Jesus, and he wants others to have that same level of commitment. This is tough to swallow, but Paul says we must not wait until we understand all of God's game plan. We must live up to what we do understand and trust Him to give us the rest in His time. To take up our cross daily requires maturity and dedication. Sure it's tough, but if we hold nothing back and keep pressing on, God will help us get through our challenges.

Lord, help me stick to Your game plan even when the times are tough. Keep me focused today on the truths I understand. Give me the strength to take up my cross each day. Amen.

Home Field Advantage

"These words that I am giving you today are to be in your heart. Repeat them to your children. Talk about them when you sit in your house and when you walk along the road, when you lie down and when you get up." Deuteronomy 6:6-8

I have never seen two baseball parks exactly the same. This makes every game unique and often leads to some very unusual developments. Distances down the baselines can be vastly different, and sometimes the walls jut out in all kinds of unusual angles. The home team usually fields balls in the corners and off the walls routinely while the visiting team looks like a Little League team. Baseball has remained the same game over the years, yet every game is different in its own way. The ball can take some crazy bounces, and the home team often has a huge advantage simply because they know the details of the ballpark.

Have you ever considered that as coaches, God expects us to establish a home-field advantage for our athletes? Think of the endless opportunities we have to develop our athletes spiritually and provide them a place to receive encouragement and support. Scripture talks about the heart of a father, but I think it applies just as much to the heart of a coach. If we want to give our athletes an advantage and put them on the right path toward God, we have to be willing to walk the pathway ourselves. Our players need to see us following God as we talk to them about doing the same thing. We need to be involved in their lives and have our eyes open to look for those teachable moments. It's our job to coach them, but it's also our responsibility to love them and be their biggest fan. As coaches, we are preparing our athletes for something much bigger than a game; we are preparing them for life. Like a baseball, life often takes a crazy hop, but if we teach our players to love, obey and serve God, it will make a huge difference in their lives.

Thank You Father for putting me in a position to impact the lives of others. May I never forget the opportunity You have given me to impact my athletes for eternity and not just a season. Amen.

Day by Day

"May the Lord be praised! Day after day He bears our burdens; God is our salvation." Psalms 68:19

There are no shortcuts in the arena of sports. Coaches and athletes learn quickly that coupling high expectations and a lack of daily effort is a recipe for failure. One of the great lessons sports teaches us is that it takes a daily commitment to get better. We have all seen athletes with great physical talent fail to reach their potential because they lack the desire to pay the daily price necessary for improvement. A recent trip to the gym reminded me this principle is true in most every area of our lives. Looking around the room, I saw men and women in their seventies or even eighties lifting weights, and using treadmills or elliptical machines. Why would senior adults make an effort to work out on a daily basis? My explanation is that it makes them feel better physically and mentally. They have learned the secret of making a daily commitment to their health. I guess that their personal lives reflect their efforts. I bet they would tell us they are happier, healthier and enjoy life more than if they simply stayed home.

Daily commitment is important in our spiritual growth too. I always feel better when I spend time with God on a daily basis. I look forward to my regular talks with God, not just in the morning or evening, but any time during the day. Just knowing God is always there and He knows my every need is a daily comfort. I have also learned it's worth the effort and essential to my spiritual development to spend time in God's Word on a daily basis. When I do, I never fail to mine that special nugget God has put there just for me. God has committed to us too. He always makes Himself available; He is always there for us. He never takes a day off or goes on vacation. God is like a caring father, always there to care for His children.

Heavenly Father, You love us more than we could ever imagine. Teach us to seek You daily. Help us grow in Your love daily. Convict us to share Your love with others daily. Amen.

No Man's Land

"So, because you are lukewarm, and neither hot nor cold, I am going to vomit you out of My mouth." Revelation 3:16

Many of us grew up with Wheaties, the cereal advertised as the breakfast of champions. When an athlete's picture appeared on the front of the Wheaties box, you knew he or she had arrived. Recently, Wheaties has fallen on hard times. There are always reasons products lose popularity, but the experts say the reason is simple; Wheaties is living in "no man's land." Marketers are saying, "Wheaties isn't healthy enough for the Fiber One crowd and isn't bad enough for the Frosted Flake crowd. By not positioning itself firmly in any camp—not quite the health food, not quite the fun food—it reaches no one." It's not just cereal that falls into this category. This can easily happen to people and especially people of faith.

Coaches, athletes, donors, and fans are challenged to give everything they have to the success of the program. We get a great example in Revelation as we see the church at Laodicea being ripped for its casual indifference to their faith. They are described as lukewarm. There was enough there for people to think it was a church of God, but when the outward appearance was taken away, a church filled with pride, ignorance, self-sufficiency, and complacency was revealed. Before we start coming down too hard on those filling the pews at Laodicea, how about us? We wear a cross around our neck and put the church magnet on our car, but who are we when we go below the surface of those outward appearances? How often are we lukewarm and how often do we find ourselves standing in no man's land? God is very clear in His disapproval of that kind of faith. Anyone with a lukewarm faith is unlikely to find their picture on a box of Wheaties; neither will they find themselves in God's good favor.

Heavenly Father, I want to be all in for You. Teach me to go beyond the appearances of faith and seek You with everything I have. Amen.

Hand and Glove

"Remain in Me, and I in you, just as a branch is unable to produce fruit by itself unless it remains on the vine, so neither can you unless you remain in Me." John 15:4

Do you remember your first new baseball glove? Mine was a genuine Tony Taylor I purchased when I was eight years old. It was awesome! It rarely left my hand during the day, and each night I would rub it down with a generous application of saddle soap to soften the leather. To help shape the glove's pocket, I would put a baseball in the center and pull it tight with my Sunday belt. This was the belt I wore for special occasions, so it was certainly appropriate. Then my glove and I would go to bed for the night. I knew this glove was going to make me a better player, and my confidence reached an all-time high. As time passed, I learned the glove wasn't going to improve my game all that much; the truth was the glove was only as good as the hand that went inside.

We can easily apply this principle to our Christian lives. My glove was a great glove, but its ability was limited. Without a skillful hand inside, the glove could not do what it was designed to do. If we think of ourselves as baseball gloves, our ability is limited without God's masterful hand working inside us. Jesus said we couldn't accomplish anything unless we are connected to our Heavenly Father. We may look productive on our own, but we have little hope of accomplishing what we were designed to do unless we stay connected to Him. We then trust God to use our gifts and talents according to His Will. Our challenge is to allow God to keep His skillful hand connected to our inconsistent lives.

Heavenly Father, thank You for the simple lessons of youth. Thank You for helping me understand that when I allow You to be the hand in my glove, You can use me to accomplish great things. Amen.

Hard Headed

"Anyone who ignores instruction despises himself, but whoever listens to correction acquires good sense." Proverbs 15:32

There is a story of a battleship on exercise at sea in bad weather. The captain was on the bridge, and the conditions were foggy. Just after dark, the lookout spotted a light on the starboard side. The captain asked if it was steady or moving. The lookout replied the light was steady, meaning they were on direct collision course with that ship! The captain ordered the lookout to signal the other ship, "Change course 20 degrees; we are on collision course." The signal came back, "Advisable for you to change course." The captain signaled, "I am the captain; change course 20 degrees." "I am a seaman second class; you had better change course 20 degrees" came the reply. The captain was furious and sent back this response: "I am a battleship; change course!" Back came the signal, "I am a lighthouse; your call."

What a great story for us as coaches. It's easy to become hard-headed and stubborn. After all, we are in charge, and we know the direction we need to be going. Too often, we get caught up in our passion for the job and neglect the advice and counsel of others. As we see it, the situation requires more determination and persistence. In truth, we may need a better understanding and perspective of the situation. Proverbs 15:32 reminds us that when we fail to listen to godly instruction, we are heading for danger. Stubbornness and ignorance can easily shipwreck our plans as well as our careers. God wants what is best for us; not only should we seek His counsel, but we should also follow it.

Heavenly Father, You are the great counselor. Teach me Your ways. Strip me of my pride and self-centeredness. Give me the wisdom and desire to follow You. Amen.

What are you Thinking?

"For as he thinks within himself, so he is." Proverbs 23:7

Every action, good or bad, begins as a simple thought. Coaches are busy! Most of us are so busy that we don't take the time to stop and think through our actions. Thinking is important! As coaches, we are always stressing the importance of fundamentals with our players, but often we forget to practice what we preach. Thinking should be fundamental in all we do. Instead of taking control of our thoughts, all too often we let them control, going wherever they want to go. That can get us into big trouble. The following words come from a Chinese proverb (author unknown):

> Be careful of your thoughts,
> for your thoughts become your words.
> Be careful of your words,
> for your words become your actions.
> Be careful of your actions,
> for your actions become your habits.
> Be careful of your habits,
> for your habits become your character.
> Be careful of your character,
> for your character becomes your destiny!

Lord, direct my thinking today. Help me understand the thoughts I have today are likely to be the actions I carry out tomorrow. Amen.

A Radical Approach

"Do not be conformed to this age, but be transformed, by the renewing of your mind, so that you may discern what is the good, pleasing, and perfect will of God." Romans 12:2

Dick Fosbury turned the track and field world on its ear during the 1968 Olympics in Mexico City. For the first time, millions of viewers watched in amazement as the high jump technique known as the Fosbury Flop was revealed. Using his back-first method, Fosbury won the gold medal in exciting fashion with a jump of 7 feet, 4 ¼ inches. While Fosbury's style was unusual, high jump rules simply say that athletes must jump off one foot on takeoff. There is no rule on how a competitor crosses the bar, as long as they go over it. What seemed like a radical idea was soon being copied and became the preferred style for high jumpers everywhere. In the 1972 Olympics, twenty-eight of the forty competitors used the Fosbury Flop. By 1980, thirteen of the sixteen Olympic finalists used it. Of the thirty-six Olympic medalists in the high jump from 1972-2000, thirty-four used the method, and today it is the most popular high jumping technique of elite competitors. What seemed like a radical idea is now the accepted way of doing things.

The world will try to squeeze us into its mold; nonconformists are not welcome. Jesus Christ came into the world and modeled a radical way to live. His sacrifice on the cross delivered us from the world and its way of doing things. As believers, the world is crucified to us, and we are crucified to the world. When we put our complete trust in Jesus Christ, our lives are transformed. We begin to think Godly thoughts, we seek His guidance and we begin to understand His love as we live in His will. This radical approach modeled by Jesus Christ over three thousand years ago is still available today. Do you believe it? Are you living it?

Heavenly Father, thank You for showing us a radical way to live our lives through Your Son Jesus Christ. Today, help me seek Your ways and not the ways of this world. Amen.

Words

"There is one who speaks rashly, like a piercing sword; but the tongue of the wise brings healing." Proverbs 12:18

Words are powerful! Words can build up or tear down. As coaches, the words we use to communicate with others say a great deal about our character. Steve Alford played basketball under the legendary Bobby Knight at Indiana University. He had this to say about Knight's language, "The worst part was the profanity. I knew the words but had never heard them in such abundance and with so much fury behind them. It was like a punch in the stomach."

Profanity is not appropriate in any situation. It is a lazy way of trying to get our point across and shows we have a very limited vocabulary. Proverbs 12:18 says our tongues can be like swords, slashing away at others, cutting and causing great pain. When we use profanity, gossip, brag or talk without thinking first, we do not honor God. We are to hold our tongues and guard our lips. Our silence can keep us from embarrassing ourselves and may even make others think we are smarter than we are. The kind of words we use is our choice! If they are not encouraging and lifting others up, some changes need to be made. Ask God for forgiveness and commit to using words that are pleasant, healing and soaked with love. You will like the difference, and others will too.

Heavenly Father, teach me the power of my words and thoughts. May they always be pleasing to You and honor You in every way. Amen.

Strength

"When a king's face lights up, there is life; his favor is like a cloud with spring rain." Proverbs 16:15

Legendary coach Vince Lombardi once said, "The strength of the group is the strength of the leader." By the very nature of being called Coach, we find ourselves in a position of leadership. Leaders must be able to make tough decisions and be prepared to sacrifice popularity for results. Doing the right thing is not always the easy thing. I can remember a coaching peer often saying, "If you can't stand the heat, get out of the kitchen." Effective leaders and coaches learn to hang in there, knowing that in time, the kitchen will cool down. As leaders, it is critical we stay calm, make good decisions and set the proper example.

King Solomon was a very wise man. He was very aware of the pitfalls of leadership and did not want to see a new generation of leaders repeat past mistakes. Proverbs 16:15 reminds us that leaders willing to do the right thing, regardless of the heat, will experience great joy when all is said and done. The resulting happiness on our face will be a comfort to those we lead. They will see us as competent leaders who can be trusted because we are centered in Christ Jesus. Learning to follow Jesus is the key to our becoming a leader worthy of following.

Heavenly Father, give me the strength to be a leader today. Give me the wisdom to see what must be done and the courage to do it. Amen.

Tested

"Therefore, when Jesus looked up and noticed a huge crowd coming toward Him, He asked Philip, 'Where will we buy bread so these people can eat?' He asked this to test him, for He Himself knew what He was going to do." John 6:5-6

Being tested is a by product of participating in sports. If we coach, we will be tested. Our opponent may look unbeatable on film, a rash of injuries may not allow us to field our best team or we could be questioning our own ability to lead. In the movie *Facing the Giants*, head football coach Grant Taylor and his team were being tested. A new season was about to begin. The team's best running back had transferred to another school and frustration was creeping into the attitudes of the coaches and players. In a pivotal scene, Coach Taylor tested a star player, who was also a team leader. The player was challenged to get on all fours, and with another player on his back, crawl as far as possible. Coach Taylor asked this question, "Can I count on you to give your absolute best?" Saying yes, the player proceeded to crawl the entire length of the football field. What seemed to be impossible had been achieved.

Jesus was tested when more than 5,000 men, women, and children came to hear Him speak and the crowd had to be fed. Even though the disciples had witnessed Jesus perform thousands of miracles, they could not understand how this was going to happen. Jesus not only fed the entire crowd, but there were plenty of leftovers. A lack of faith had been exposed, and the disciples realized God was more than enough to overcome every test. What about you? How strong is your faith? Do you believe God is enough? Our daily challenge is to realize we can count on God, and His provision is always more than enough.

Heavenly Father, as I face the tests of today, give me Your strength. Help me see I am not alone; You are with me and You are enough. Amen.

Hold Your Tongue

"Your speech should always be gracious, seasoned with salt, so that you may know how you should answer each person." Colossians 4:6

Have you ever been guilty of shooting off your mouth before you put your brain in gear? In a recent youth league baseball game, I watched the head coach get tossed for arguing balls and strikes with the home plate umpire. Not only was he thrown out of the game, but he was also forced to leave the dugout and the stadium in full view of those in attendance. Not the best example for a group of 9-10 year olds. It was obvious the coach got caught up at the moment, and his anger spilled out. This episode reminded me of the old saying, "You don't have to attend every argument you're invited to." Angry words can't be retrieved.

The Apostle Paul tells us to speak with grace. Our words should be courteous, humble and Christ-like. When our words are seasoned with salt, they are worthwhile and lift others up. When we talk, we should choose language we would use if God were listening because He is. Our words are more important than we may realize, and angry words can have long-term consequences. What situations or people light your anger fuse? Give them to God and trust Him to help you make the necessary changes. Remember that some fights are lost even when we win. "A bulldog can whip a skunk, but it just isn't worth it."

Lord, teach me to choose my words carefully. Help me understand that my words have the ability to build up or tear down. Give me wisdom and strength to speak greatness into my players, family and friends every day. Amen.

Keeping Our Eyes on Jesus

"Therefore since we also have such a large crowd of witnesses surrounding us, let us lay aside every weight and the sin that so easily ensnares us, and run with endurance the race that lies before us, keeping our eyes on Jesus, the source and perfecter of our faith, who for the joy that lay before Him endured the cross and despised the shame, and has sat down at the right hand of God's throne." Hebrews 12:1-2

The forecast for Friday night's game is rain! To a football coach, that means making some major adjustments to the week's practice schedule. There's something about the threat of wet weather that makes us a little nervous in our preparation. In my experience, the threat of poor weather conditions usually forces me to think less about game planning for the opponent and more about my own team's execution. Being solid in the fundamentals of blocking and tackling or simply holding on to the football take on a greater importance when playing on a soggy field. This certainly isn't all bad. Isn't it interesting that a little rain can force us to shift our focus back to where it should have been all along?

I have experienced this same principle in my spiritual walk. Too often I become consumed with everything happening around me. I'm trying to be a good spouse and parent. I'm working hard to have quality quiet time with the Lord and pay the bills. Sometimes it's just more than I can handle, and the weight is slowing me down. In times like these, God always seems to send a little rain to help me readjust my focus. The soggy field He sends my way usually forces me to think less about the big picture and more about the fundamentals necessary to be in a relationship with Him. To put it in simple terms, it might take a little rain to help get your eyes back on Jesus. If that's what it takes, I say, "Bring it on!"

Heavenly Father, forgive me for losing focus of what is really important, being in relationship with You. Thank You for the rain that forces me to turn my eyes back to You. Amen.

Joy

"You reveal the path of life to me; in Your presence is abundant joy; in Your right hand are eternal pleasures." Psalm 16:11

Can you remember the most joyful celebration you've ever witnessed? Maybe it was celebrating a state championship or an unexpected win over a superior opponent. It could have been witnessing one of your athletes accomplish a feat that they, and maybe you too, thought was impossible. What made that moment so joyful? Sports are always providing us with joyful moments. An overwhelming excitement results when we succeed. Success usually brings happiness to athletes, coaches, and fans, but are joy and happiness the same thing?

The Apostle Paul teaches us a great deal about joy. If anyone had a reason not to be joyful, it might be Paul. He was beaten and stoned. Three times he was shipwrecked. His ministry brought him hunger, thirst, imprisonment and great personal hardship. Paul remained upbeat and positive. Like Paul, if we are walking close to God, we can have joy in our hearts no matter what is happening to us or around us. Joy is not based on emotional feelings or events. It's an ongoing certainty and feeling of peace that no matter what life throws at us, God is still in control. We must never forget God loves us more than we can comprehend, and His love is unconditional. Let's focus on being joyful in all circumstances. Let's pray for the courage and commitment to make joy part of our daily lives.

Father God, I pray today for joy over happiness. Help me see that joy comes from walking with You and not from the successes of this world. Help me to keep my focus on You. Amen.

Undefeated

"Now the sting of death is sin, and the power of sin is the law. But thanks be to God, who gives us the victory through our Lord Jesus Christ." 1 Corinthians 15:56-57

In the world of sport, each new season brings excitement and hope. The previous season is history, and we all get a fresh start. The great news is that everyone is undefeated! As the season plays out, however, very few teams can win them all. Sometimes the other team is better, and there are some nights the ball simply does not bounce our way. To go undefeated is a rare and amazing experience. The very nature of sport requires us to record our losses and deal with them in our way.

If life were a sports contest, we would rack up our share of losses along the way. Why? Because we are sinful. As hard as we may try, we sin, and the Bible says the result of sin is death. Since God is sinless, that leaves us in a serious predicament. We can't be with God in our sin. This is where Jesus enters the game on our behalf. He took on our sin and died an agonizing death on the cross so we could stay in the game. Satan seemed to be victorious at the cross of Jesus, but God turned Satan's apparent victory into defeat when Jesus rose from the dead. Sin and death are no matches for God has and always will win! God has and always will be undefeated!

Heavenly Father, thank You for giving me a way to be on Your team. Thank You for Your amazing love demonstrated at the cross. Help me live out my life for You and share Your love with others. Amen.

Distractions

"Let your eyes look forward; fix your gaze straight ahead." Proverbs 4:25

Regardless of the level you coach, teaching athletes to minimize distractions is important. Anyone who has ever coached youth sports knows what I'm talking about. I remember a baseball game in which two of my eight-year-old players got into a fight in the dugout, arguing over who was going to put on the extra set of catcher's gear. Another day, I almost blew a gasket when at the most critical point of a big game I observed my right-fielder sitting on the ground building dirt castles! Distractions for athletes come in many forms: trash talking from the opponent, poor weather conditions, parents trying to coach from the stands, opposing fans, fear of making a mistake, and as previously mentioned, even catcher's equipment and dirt. What often keeps our athletes from reaching their peak performance is not that they stop focusing but that they focus their attention on the wrong things. As coaches, we must be prepared to help our athletes stay focused on the right things.

Distractions are also common in everyday life. We get caught in traffic, our children get sick and we get that unexpected phone call or text at just the wrong time. For coaches, there is never a shortage of free advice being offered, reminding us what we could have done or should have done in last night's game. Staying focused on the right things is something for which we must be prepared. Proverbs is filled with practical advice on dealing with the everyday problems we face. Proverbs 4:25 reminds us to walk with a single purpose. We are to look straight ahead, keeping our eyes on Jesus. We are to guard ourselves against distractions that might take us away from that purpose. Keeping our focus on Jesus is always the right thing! Are you distracted today? Get into God's Word and refocus.

Heavenly Father, I ask Your forgiveness for being so easily distracted. Too often my eyes and ears are focused on things that are simply not important. Help me focus today. Give me Your strength as I strive to keep my eyes on Your Son, Jesus Christ. Amen.

Faith

"Stephen, full of grace and power, was performing great wonders and signs among the people." Acts 6:8

Charles Blondin was a great French acrobat who became a legend by crossing the entire width of Niagara Falls on a tightrope. He first did it pushing a wheelbarrow, another time blindfolded, and yet another walking backward. Blondin's greatest achievement, however, was crossing the falls with another man on his back. As I think about this feat, I know it was difficult for Blondin, but what about the man who was willing to climb on his back for the most unbelievable ride of his life? That man was Blondin's manager, Harry Colcord. While history doesn't say a great deal about Colcord, we do know one thing—he had enough faith in the acrobat to put his life in Blondin's hands.

In Acts 6, we are introduced to a man called Stephen. He was one of the men appointed by the apostles to handle the daily affairs of the church. God had great faith in Stephen and gave him the ability to do miracles and preach. Stephen was later killed because he refused to turn away from his faith in God. As coaches, many people put their faith in us each day: administrators, parents, athletes, and peers, just to mention a few. In his book, *Becoming a Person of Influence,* John Maxwell gives his readers four facts about faith: "most people don't have faith in themselves; most people don't have someone who has faith in them; most people can tell when someone has faith in them, and most people will do anything to live up to our faith in them." Having faith in others takes more than words or feelings about them. We have to back it up with our actions. Be a believer in the people around you today, and they will bloom right before your eyes.

Heavenly Father, You are a faithful God. You have been with me in the past, are with me in the present and will be with me in the future. Lord, help me to be faithful to those You have called me to serve today. In Jesus name I pray. Amen.

Integrity

"Little children, we must not love in word or speech, but in deed and truth."
1 John 3:18

Before Arnold Palmer won the Masters in 1960, he agreed to play in an exhibition the week following the Masters. After winning the tournament, Palmer's agent received a call from the organizers of the event. They assumed Palmer would either not be coming or his fee would be significantly more. What would Palmer do? He told them he would not only honor his commitment, but he would also do another event for them the next year for the same price. Palmer explained that they wanted him long before he had won a major championship. His circumstances had changed, but his integrity was still evident.

People say Arnold Palmer never changed, despite his wealth and popularity. Palmer obviously received a firm foundation early in life that stayed with him as money and fame came his way. What about us? Do we honor our word and our commitments, or do we sometimes suffer short-term memory? God's Word reminds us that we have to "walk the walk," not just "talk the talk." Would someone be able to look at us and know we follow Jesus Christ without us telling them? Our challenge is to focus on being men and women of action, not just words.

Heavenly Father, thank You for Your Word that speaks truth into our world. Guide me today and make my actions stronger than my words. Amen.

Fear

"My spirit is weak within me; my heart is overcome with dismay." Psalm 143:4

Spiders, flying, heights, storms and snakes are only a few of the fears that paralyze some of us. Others include loneliness, rejection, fear of the unknown and fear of failure. We all face fears of some kind. Fear is defined as an emotion caused by a perceived threat which leads to a change in behavior such as running away, hiding, or freezing. A recent trip to the Grand Canyon brought me face to face with my fear of heights. Standing on the trail looking out into the vastness of the canyon below not only made me weak in the knees, but it also froze me in my tracks. What do we do with fear when it shows up on our front door? If fear is an emotion, it can be changed, but it doesn't just happen. Change comes only as the result of deliberate action. As I continued my trip hiking national parks in Utah, I found myself being intentional about confronting my fear. With a little prayer, a personal desire to take a few risks, and the encouragement of others, I was able to enjoy my experience and feel better about myself.

Scripture talks a great deal about fear. David was losing all hope, caught up in his fear and deep depression. He was hiding in caves from King Saul, who was trying to kill him. Like being in prison, David was trapped, and the chances of getting out of the mess seemed futile. Didn't anyone care? In his desperation, David remembers God's previous acts of love and faithfulness. He cries out and tells God how he feels. David turns himself over to God's guidance and puts his complete trust in God's hands. He asks God to direct his life and finds hope in the process. What is your fear today: a losing record, what others think, a failing marriage, finances? Why not try David's approach and tell God your true feelings? Put your fear in God's hands, and let Him guide your path.

Heavenly Father, fear and timidity do not come from You. Hear my cry today and deliver me from my fears. I put my complete trust in You. Amen.

Which Way Do I Go?

"'Look', the attendant said, 'there's a man of God in this city who is highly respected; everything he says is sure to come true. Let's go there now. Maybe he'll tell us which way we should go.'" 1 Samuel 9:6

Yogi Berra was a Hall of Fame baseball player with a Hall of Fame wit. He had a gift for saying the smartest things in the funniest ways. As a result, Yogi became one of America's most beloved philosophers. Berra played for one of the greatest dynasties in baseball history, the New York Yankees. He played on ten world championship teams and won the American League Most Valuable Player Award three times. Even with these great team and individual accomplishments, Berra is best known for his Yogi-isms. He had a knack for saying something that made no sense, yet interpreted with a little perspective could make perfect sense. Once Berra was giving his friend and fellow baseball player, Joe Garagiola, directions on how to get to his home. After giving numerous landmarks and turns, he concluded by saying, "And when you come to the fork in the road, take it." I can only imagine the head scratching that took place with those instructions; I hope Garagiola made it.

If we're honest with ourselves, Yogi's wisdom could also apply to our spiritual lives. I can recall many times in my life when I didn't know exactly where to go or which direction to take. As coaches, how often are we faced with making decisions on the fly or with very little information? Coaching can be a tough profession, and I have seen many coaches make a wrong turn that cost them their job, their family or their reputation. We have to be very careful, stay focused and keep our eyes on Jesus at all times. We can always trust Him to guide us in those moments of doubt.

Heavenly Father, help me make good decisions today. Give me the wisdom to seek Your guidance in all I do. Amen.

Frustration

"So we must not get tired of doing good, for we will reap at the proper time if we don't give up." Galatians 6:9

It's a common practice for me to go to the sports section on Friday mornings to check out the high school football matchups for the evening. Normally, I'm looking for the best games involving undefeated teams or contests that involve a great offense going against a great defense. While going through this process recently, my attention was diverted to an article highlighting a game between two 0-4 teams. The story stated a painful but obvious fact. When the night was over, one of those teams was still going to be winless. As a coach I have been there and it's frustrating riding home on a Friday night with a 0-5 team. The critical question to be answered when we find ourselves in that situation is this: "How are we going to deal with it?" If frustration is already here, panic can't be far away. One of my standard lines when I offer encouragement to frustrated coaches is this: "Coach, you're doing it the right way, just keep doing it."

Coaching is a lifestyle filled with ups and downs. When we're losing, it's easy to panic and make changes for all the wrong reasons. Instead of teaching our players, we start yelling at them. We make practices longer and more difficult and wonder why our players aren't responding. We even begin to listen to some of the suggestions from those outside the team and are tempted to drift away from everything we stand for as a person and a coach. In Galatians 6:9, Paul is encouraging us to not get frustrated when the rewards aren't immediate. A farmer doesn't harvest a field of wheat the day after he puts the seed in the ground. When we are doing it the right way, the rewards are guaranteed. God promises they will come in due season. Remember that 0-5 team I mentioned earlier; they finished 5-5. Coach, you're doing it the right way; just keep doing it!

Heavenly Father, thank You for not giving up on me. Help me today to control my frustration. Help me see the bigger picture. Give me the strength to keep doing it the right way. Amen.

Distractions

"So we do not focus on what is seen, but on what is unseen. For what is seen is temporary, but what is unseen is eternal." 2 Corinthians 4:18

One of the great problems in leadership is becoming distracted. How often as coaches do we find ourselves getting off the main road and meandering down rabbit trails? When we're focused and our vision is clear, we become like a racehorse in the Kentucky Derby with blinders on. We are zoned in! In his book *The Legend of Bear Bryant*, Mickey Herskowitz described the famed Alabama football coach's vision. "Coach Bryant could always focus on something with both eyes and still find a third eye to be looking at himself while he was doing it." How many times could we use a third eye? Coach Bryant avoided distractions, and he stressed the right priorities: faith, family, education and then winning football games.

Life will often distract us and take us off the main road. Personal illness, losing seasons, or the failure to save that athlete you poured your heart into, are events that can derail us. Our challenge is to see beyond the present and focus on the big picture. Our troubles shouldn't cause us to lose faith or shatter our vision. There are even some benefits to going through hard times. They can keep us from becoming prideful. They cause us to look beyond this life. They can give us the opportunity to grow our faith and share that faith with others. Paul does his best to encourage us by reminding us that this life is not all there is. As a follower of Jesus Christ, we are promised so much more; we are promised life after death! Knowing we will live forever with God in a place without sin and suffering can help us live above the pain we face in this life.

Heavenly Father, keep me focused today. Help me keep my eyes on the big picture as I deal with the constant distractions that come my way. I pray this in Jesus name. Amen.

Character Counts

"...you are being renewed in the spirit of your minds; you put on the new man, the one created according to God's (likeness) in righteousness and purity of truth." Ephesians 4:23-24

There is an ongoing debate in our nation about the issue of leadership and character. In the realm of politics, it appears that if polls and the economy are good, then character doesn't matter. As coaches, however, most of us adhere to the idea that good character is essential to good leadership. The debate is real, so what's the answer? Speaking at a conference, former Oklahoma congressman J.C. Watts asked his audience some interesting questions. "How many of you wives think the character of your husband is important?" Every hand in the room went up. Then he asked, "How many of you husbands think the character of your wife is important?" Again, one hundred percent of the hands were raised. "Then tell me the character of our leaders is not important!" Watts said. "You can no more have leadership without character than you can have water without the wet."

When we decide to live our lives for Jesus, we don't become perfect, but there should be a dramatic change! Our old way of life is in the past. As believers, we are transformed and take on a new nature. We put our old ways behind us like old clothes being thrown away. When we decide to accept Christ's gift of salvation, it's both a one-time decision and a daily commitment. We are not driven by desire and impulse. We put on a new nature, head in a new direction and have a new way of thinking that comes from the Holy Spirit. Being men and women of good character is a key ingredient of this glorious transformation.

Heavenly Father, thank You for changing my life. Thank You for the opportunity to positively impact lives. Help me embrace this challenge today and be a coach of character. Amen.

Vision

"Where there is no vision, the people are unrestrained...." Proverbs 29:18

Longtime Alabama head football coach Paul "Bear" Bryant knew what vision was all about. In his book *Bear Bryant on Leadership,* Pat Williams says, "Bryant saw the future before it arrived. He saw over the horizon before others even opened their eyes. He saw victory parades in the streets and facilities already built. He even saw his team's national championship trophies glistening in the light before they were won." In a career that covered thirty-eight years, Bryant's teams won 323 games and six national championships. Coach Bryant's vision went beyond Xs and Os, game plans and wins and losses. His vision included academics, life skills for his athletes, media and sports publicity and having the best athletic facilities in the nation. He even established a scholarship program for 700 children of former players to attend the University of Alabama.

Vision is a bridge between the present and the future. Without it, we sway from one thing to another. A lack of vision causes us to settle for the path of least resistance in each decision we make. Vision is not only what we see but also the way we see. There is an old story about three bricklayers that helps us understand proper vision. "There were three bricklayers working beside each other on a wall. Someone came up to the first one and said, 'What are you doing?' 'What's it look like I'm doing?' he replied sarcastically. 'I'm laying bricks!' The man asked the next guy on the wall what he was doing. He said, 'Can't you see what I'm doing? I'm building a wall.' Then the last man was asked what he was doing. He enthusiastically exclaimed, 'I'm building a great cathedral for God!'" Vision causes people to love their work because they can see the big picture. Is your vision a little blurred? To see clearly, we must not only know God's ways but also keep His rules. If we could only envision what God sees for each of us; My guess is that it's not a brick or a wall, but a great cathedral for Him.

Heavenly Father, You are a God of vision. Help me understand that I'm a part of Your vision. Open my eyes today to see the vision You have for me and to carry it out. Amen.

To Know Him

"My goal is to know Him and the power of His resurrection and the fellowship of His sufferings, being conformed to His death." Philippians 3:10

To compete in the world of athletics takes motivation and drive. As coaches, we invest countless hours training our athletes to perform at the highest level possible. What is our payoff? Why do we do it? It could be a state championship or simply a winning season. It might be a Coach of the Year award or gaining respect for the program in the community. While these can be worthy goals, they are what we could call surface desires or earthly trophies. We can spend our entire life collecting earthly trophies. It might be a trophy car, a trophy house, a trophy spouse or a trophy coaching position. It can be easy for us to focus on surface desires, which seldom satisfy us in the long run.

The Apostle Paul had a lot of trophies: power, influence, prestige, money, significance and success. He was living the good life and performing at the top of his game. Paul's problem, however, was that his desires were misplaced. He was aggressively persecuting Jesus and his followers. When Paul met Jesus on the road to Damascus, his focus changed forever. His new desire and focus were to know Jesus and be on His team. Paul's motivation shifted from earthly trophies to heavenly trophies, and he never turned back. Our challenge is to take a closer look at our present desires and determine whether they fall into the category of temporary or eternal rewards. Are we collecting earthly trophies or heavenly trophies?

Heavenly Father, You know me better than I know myself. As I go about the work You have called me to do, give me a true perspective of what is really important. Help me strive for the trophies that have eternal value. In Jesus name. Amen.

Be Thankful

"I will praise God's name with song and exalt Him with thanksgiving."
Psalm 69:30

We see it so often now that we don't even give it a second thought. Following a touchdown the jubilant football player goes into his private victory celebration. Just when we think we have seen all the dances and stunts that could be performed, someone takes it to another level. It now has become an outrageous contest to see who can draw the most attention to themselves. I might be thinking old school here, but wouldn't it be nice if just once the player went back and thanked everyone who made the touchdown possible! High fives for the linemen who made the blocks, slaps on the back for the coaches who called the play and acknowledgment to the fans who gave their money and time to attend the game. All too often, players forget about all the people who made it possible for them to get into the end zone in the first place.

Sometimes as coaches, we too forget to thank those who help us do what we do. Our spouses and good friends who love us and encourage us even in the darkest times, the assistant coaches who get in the foxhole with us and fight the battles with us each day, our players who trust us to do what is best for them and the team, our administrators who hired us to model good character and integrity on and off the field, and most of all, our God, deserve our gratitude. It's God who gave us our abilities and talents, and we are to use them to glorify Him. Our challenge is to be thankful for all those we serve as well as those who serve us. The next time we want to say, "Hey everyone; look at me; look what I did," let's remember those who helped us get where we are.

Heavenly Father, everything comes from You, and I am thankful. Thank You for those people You have put around me, who love me and encourage me. Help me to never take these gifts for granted. Amen.

Growth

"Brothers, I do not consider myself to have taken hold of it. But one thing I do: forgetting what is behind and reaching forward to what is ahead." Philippians 3:13

As a recreational runner for over forty years, I have learned a great deal about myself. I lost twenty-five pounds during Army basic training and liked the way I felt and looked. As the years rolled by and my professional responsibilities grew, I desperately needed the hour of solitude my daily runs provided. Running gave me the time to unwind, reflect and think. I truly believe those runs made me a better teacher and coach, a better husband and father, and a stronger person of faith. Not only was running providing physical benefits, but I was also growing mentally and spiritually as well. In my fifties, I went through a time of competitive running. I learned some valuable lessons. Someone is always faster! I also realized the race was more about me than the competition. I learned to run my race and celebrate my victories. Today, I enjoy the fellowship of my running friends. We discuss the world's problems, test one another with trivia and enjoy a lot of good laughter.

In many ways, my spiritual journey has paralleled my journey as a runner. In the early years, I went to church because my parents expected me to be there. After surrendering my life to Jesus, I wanted more. I realized that to grow in my relationship with Christ, I had to do some work. As I read and studied my Bible, I discovered I needed that quiet time with Him. Like running, this time allowed me to unwind, reflect and think. I was growing daily, and I liked the person God was helping me become more than I did the old me. My spiritual goal is to be a little more like Jesus today than I was yesterday.

Heavenly Father, thank You for the gifts You have given me. Help me use them in service to others, and help me to be a little more like Your Son Jesus at the end of the day than I was at the beginning. Amen.

Discipleship

"Then Jesus came near and said to them, 'All authority in heaven and on earth has been given to me. Therefore go and make disciples of all nations, baptizing them in the name of the Father and the Son of the Holy Spirit, and teaching them to obey everything I have commanded you. And surely I am with you always, to the end of the age.'" Matthew 28:18-20

Where has the time gone? Has it been more than forty years since I started coaching? As I think back over my coaching career, there are many people who have poured into me with encouragement and guidance. Coach Babb, you gave me my first coaching job at Greenwood High School. You taught me to take pride in doing the little things. My first head coaching job was at Pelion High School. The people of that community had never had a football team. You taught me how special a small town can be, and when you pull together for something you want great things can happen. Coach Daye at Brookland-Cayce High School taught me that when life hits you in the face, you say thanks and move on. At Columbia High School, Coach Charlie Macaluso modeled the value of doing the best you can do one day at a time. Through these men and experiences, I was discipled.

Discipleship is often a meaningless word to us, but Jesus gave us marching orders from God in the Great Commission. Jesus commanded us to make disciples and to teach them to obey everything He taught. That should get us pumped! We should get out of bed each morning excited about the opportunity to tell people about Jesus, to make disciples for the Lord and to be true disciples ourselves. However, too often we look at worldly areas to measure our success. If we want to make a difference in the lives of others, we need to be intentional in the area of discipleship. Take a moment to reflect on the people who have discipled you over the years. Then, truly commit yourself to making disciples of those you work with and meet each day.

Heavenly Father, thank You for showing me the way and for putting people in my life to keep me on the right path. Make me mindful today of the responsibility I have to disciple others. Amen.

The "Want"

"More than that, I also consider everything to be a loss in view of the surpassing value of knowing Christ Jesus my Lord. Because of Him, I have suffered the loss of all things and consider them filth, so that I may gain Christ."
Philippians 3:8

Coaches desire great things for themselves and the athletes they teach. This desire drives them to compete, pursue and strive toward their ultimate goal of the season. This could be called the want to achieve. In team sports, the wants of individual players don't always match up with the wants of the team. The challenge for coaches is to get the entire team to want the same thing and focus on that goal all season long.

The Apostle Paul was single-minded. His desire or want in life was much different from most others of his time. He didn't value the trophies and recognition others desired. Paul's sole want was to "gain Christ." His only desire was to know Jesus Christ better and better with each passing day. He did not let his circumstances, the people around him or an uncertain future get in the way of the number one object of his desire—Jesus Christ. Every day, Paul shared his desire with others and prayed they would join him. The want can be powerful! Paul knew what he wanted, and his focus never wavered. What is the greatest want in your faith journey? What price are you willing to pay to achieve it?

Heavenly Father, teach me Your ways and give me the desire to pursue Your will for my life today and every day. Amen.

Keeping It Simple

"He first found his brother Simon and told him, 'We have found the Messiah!' (which means "Anointed One"), and he brought (Simon) to Jesus." John 1:41

Most successful coaches have learned the art of effective communication. Coaches are teachers in the truest sense, but our classrooms look a little different. We teach on grassy fields, hardwood courts and synthetic tracks instead of rooms lined with desks, tables and chairs. In communicating with our athletes, coaches often make it harder than it needs to be. We take an athletic skill, break it down into multiple stages and techniques, and then try to teach it to our athletes so that they can execute it perfectly. To be blunt, coaches can take something simple and make it complicated. Before we know it, we can have our athletes thinking more and executing less. Effective coaches learn the value of keeping things simple. Charles Swindoll had this advice for pastors, and it applies to coaches as well. "If there is mist behind the pulpit, there is fog in the pew." Ever feel like your athletes were in a fog? Maybe you're making it too complicated.

I love the disciple Andrew; he understood the value of keeping his message simple. Andrew was one of the first to meet Jesus following his baptism by John the Baptist. When a person finds Jesus, he usually wants his friends and relatives to meet Him too. So Andrew finds his brother Simon and shares this simple message, "We have found the Messiah!" What a powerful message contained in only five words. Men had been waiting for the promised Christ for thousands of years, and now He was here. I can only laugh when I think about how a coach might have tried to tell it. We know one thing for sure; it would have taken more than five words! No mist, no fog, just, "We have found the Messiah!" More profound words have never been spoken.

Heavenly Father, thank You for keeping Your message simple. You made me, You love me, and You want me to spend eternity with You. Help me share these simple truths with those I teach today. Amen.

Ladders and Crowns

"For the Lord takes pleasure in His people; He adorns the humble with salvation." Psalm 149:4

Another football season is coming to a close. Teams have made their way through the regular season schedule. For the past few weeks, television has been saturated with bowl games and All-Star games. Some teams achieved great success and were crowned champions of their region or conference. Players have been named to All-American, All-Conference, and All-State teams. Many of these players will showcase their skills in games just for them. Coaches have been named Coach of the Year and nominated for various Halls of Fame. As coaches and athletes, we're always chasing crowns. Trophies, rings, plaques and medals are the crowns that often motivate us. If we're not careful, we can lose our perspective on the things that matter most. Long-time NFL coach Bobby Jackson once said, "I climbed the ladder of success almost all the way to the top, but I found that my ladder was leaning against the wrong wall."

It's all too easy for us to put our ladders against the wrong wall. The victories and awards can give us a false sense of pride. We must constantly be on guard and frequently ask ourselves why we do what we do. We should challenge ourselves regularly with this question, "Who's getting the glory?" Psalm 149 reminds us to be humble and give thanks to God for any success we might have. We need to understand the crowns of the world quickly fade away and lose their value. Few people can remember last year's champion. On the other hand, God loves us so much that He offers us a crown that will last forever, if only we commit our lives to Him. Let's give some thought to where we're going to place our ladders. Are we going to climb walls with limited value, or are we going to climb walls with eternal value?

Heavenly Father, I ask for the wisdom to place my ladders on the right walls. Help me today to see and strive for the things that have eternal value. Amen.

Take a Knee

"Be still and know that I am God! I will be honored by every nation. I will be honored throughout the world." Psalm 46:10

"Everybody take a knee!" It's not unusual for a coach to gather his or her team together following an intense drill or at the end of a difficult practice. As the athletes take a knee, they know the pace is about to change. After an extended period of constant movement and intense activity, the action stops and the focus changes. Coach commands that all eyes and ears are fixed on him or her. During the next few minutes, they can anticipate that coach is going to share something important everyone needs to hear.

I'm constantly reminded of the importance of finding time to take a knee with God. Everyone I know is busy! Careers, family and technology consume us and much of our time each day. Psalm 46:10 instructs us to "be still and know that I am God." Are you allowing God to be the center of your life? Are you spending time with Him on a daily basis? Are you reading and living out His Word? How long has it been since you took a knee and focused on what God has to tell you? Give it a try; I guarantee He's going to share something you need to hear!

Heavenly Father, You are an all-knowing counselor. Your wisdom is great. Create in me the desire to spend time with You today and every day. In Jesus name I pray, Amen.

Whatever It Takes

"Don't ask me to leave you and turn back. Wherever you go, I will go." Ruth 1:16

The match with our cross-town rival was going to be intense. The teams were evenly matched, and it would take our best effort to get the victory. In game-planning, it was decided that our opponent's best player was not going beat us. He was athletic, fast and capable of scoring from anywhere on the pitch. To take him out of his game, we decided to mark him with our best defender and make his life as miserable as possible. Our defender was given these explicit instructions, "Wherever he goes, you go!" We took the challenge one more step by telling him, "even if your man goes to the bathroom or the concession stand, you go with him." The message was clear; do whatever it takes to keep your man from determining the outcome of the match. The strategy worked to perfection. Frustrated and even angry at our tactics, this excellent player became a mess, and the victory was ours.

As coaches, we like to be around people who are committed to the task. Ruth knew about commitment and doing whatever it took to get the job done. She had married the son of a woman named Naomi and loved her very much. Naomi's husband had died, and ten years later Ruth's husband also died, leaving both women in a difficult situation. There was nothing worse than being a widow during this time because women without husbands were often taken advantage of or ignored. Naomi encouraged Ruth to look out for herself, find a new husband and move on with her life. Ruth's immediate response was "wherever you go, I will go." Ruth was willing to give up her security to care for Naomi. How did God reward Ruth for her commitment? She became a great-grandmother of King David and a direct ancestor of Jesus.

Heavenly Father, thank You for Your unwavering commitment to me. Strengthen me today Lord, to be committed to You in all I do. Give me the heart to go wherever You go and never turn back. Amen.

Fix Your Eyes

"Therefore since we also have such a large crowd of witnesses surrounding us, let us lay aside every weight and sin that easily ensnares us, and run with endurance the race that lies before us, keeping our eyes on Jesus, the source and Perfecter of our faith, who for the joy that lay before Him endured a cross and despised the shame, and has sat down at the right hand of God's throne." Hebrews 12:1-2

As coaches, we're always talking to our athletes about the need to focus. Baseball coaches remind players to keep their eyes on the ball. When teaching tackling, football coaches tell athletes to aim for the number on the front of the jersey. In basketball, coaches teach free throw shooting by telling players to focus on the front of the rim. Former NFL receiver Steve Largent was once asked what he kept his eyes on when a quarterback threw him a pass. The obvious answer was the ball, but Largent said he focused on the cross hairs formed by the seams on the football's tip. That is impossible in light of how hard NFL quarterbacks throw the ball, but Largent's answer showed the intensity of his focus.

Hebrews 12:1-2 teaches us not only the value of focus but also the importance of keeping our eyes on the right object. Too often we turn our attention to the problems in our life or the mistakes we have made in the past. The more we focus on the problems and mistakes, the more difficult it becomes to keep our eyes on Jesus Christ. Coaches don't want to see their players distracted. God doesn't want us to lose our focus either. Focus on Jesus; He is the source and protector of our faith.

Heavenly Father, help me eliminate the distractions in my life today. Give me the strength to fix my eyes on You and not my problems. Keep me focused Lord. Amen.

Anger

"David had just said, 'I guarded everything that belonged to this man in the wilderness for nothing. He was not missing anything, yet he paid me back evil for good. May God punish me, and even more if I let any of his men survive until morning.'" 1 Samuel 25:21-22

What causes you to get angry? During the 1968 French Open, Brian Barnes set a record for the most putts ever needed to sink a three-footer. After blowing an easy putt for par, Barnes tried to rake the ball back into the cup and missed. Losing total control, he hit the ball back and forth over the cup until he finally holed out. The result—a 12!!

King David knew about anger. He had protected Nabal's servants and land, which allowed the servants to work without fear and thus produce more. When David sent some of his men for a portion of the harvest, Nabal refused to give them anything. David exploded; he was ready to kill Nabal and every male in Nabal's family. Does your anger sometimes cause you to lose control? As followers of Jesus Christ, we are called to a higher standard. We are called to forgive those who anger and upset us. Sure, it's a challenge, but if we think about the forgiveness God has given us, we might be a little easier on those we feel don't deserve to be forgiven.

Heavenly Father, thank You for being a God of mercy and grace. Teach me today to be slow to anger and quick to forgive. Amen.

Knuckleballs & Knuckleheads

"I know, Lord, that a man's way of life is not his own; no one who walks determines his own steps." Jeremiah 10:23

In the game of baseball, the knuckleball is probably the hardest to pitch, hit and catch. The pitcher doesn't know where it's going when he throws it; the hitter has difficulty adjusting to the ball's random movement and the poor catcher can only try his best to knock it down as it crosses the plate. Phil Niekro made a living throwing the knuckleball during his career and earned his way into the Major League Baseball Hall of Fame. In the modern era, R. A. Dickey has somewhat mastered the knuckleball and enjoyed major league success. The knuckleball is slow by major league standards, only traveling at a speed of 60-75 miles per hour. It seems to have a mind of its own as it moves, dips and drops in every direction.

Jeremiah 10:23 reminds us that we can be a great deal like the knuckleball in our personal lives. Too often we find ourselves in trouble as a result of trying to direct our own lives. Like the knuckleball, we move this way, dip that way and flutter in every possible direction. Has your life ever been so out of control that you felt like a knucklehead? Jeremiah's message is that it doesn't have to be that way. When we surrender our lives to Jesus, our lives are no longer our own. It's no longer up to us to determine our path. Trying to direct our own lives is as hopeless as trying to direct a knuckleball. When we realize our lives are not our own and God's plans are better than anything we could imagine, we have a chance. It's about surrender—we need to surrender our will to God. He will show us the way to go and give us all the direction we need.

Lord, thank You for loving me even when I act like a knucklehead. Teach me Father to be obedient to the wisdom found in Your Word. Help me today to surrender to Your will and not my own. Amen.

Focus

"Brothers, I do not consider myself to have taken hold of it. But one thing I do: forgetting what is behind and reaching forward to what is ahead, I pursue as my goal the prize promised by God's heavenly call in Christ Jesus."
Philippians 3:13-14

As competitors, it's critical we maintain our focus. All too often we have watched coaches and athletes become content with past accomplishment. It is so easy to think we have "arrived." Media experts are always predicting the outcome of the coming season. They analyze all the data and project which teams and players will have the best season. Many of these predictions are based on how the team finished last year or how many returning players are on the current roster. It's easy for teams to get lulled into a false sense of security and take their eyes off the objective. Every year we see teams go into the season with great hopes only to fall short of those lofty expectations.

The apostle Paul warns us of this trap. He was a man of single purpose, and his focus was on one aim and ambition. Paul tells us to forget what is in the past. He is not only talking about our sins and failures but our successes as well. Too often, we think we have arrived spiritually. I'm a good Christian. I go to church; I serve others in my community; I pray. Like the athlete, we can lose our focus. When we take our eyes off Jesus, we are setting ourselves up for a huge fall. The prize we are competing for is our salvation and the opportunity to live for eternity with Christ. To obtain the prize requires not only focus but our very best effort. We must discipline ourselves to stretch, strain and strive every day to reach this goal. The prize is worth the effort.

Father, thank You for the blessings You provide each day. Keep me focused Lord, as I seek to live for You each day. Push me, prod me and stretch me to grow in Your love today. Amen.

Contentment

"I don't say this out of need, for I have learned to be content in whatever circumstances I am." Philippians 4:11

You may think the grass is greener on the other side, but if you take the time to water your grass, it would be just as green. It's a natural part of the coaching profession to be in search of bigger and better opportunities. To move up the coaching ladder, we're always in search of greener grass. Sometimes, however, we get ahead of ourselves in the process. How often do we get impatient or frustrated with our present situation and simply give up to move on to something else? How often do we find the green grass that looks so good at a distance is not nearly as green as the grass we are standing on? In our haste, it's all too easy to miss the amazing opportunities in our pasture as we gaze longingly at the distant horizon.

Although Paul is talking about contentment in his finances, this verse is easily applicable to our work. Contentment is seldom found in money, jobs or things alone. Paul encourages us to look beyond the obvious and see that contentment comes from within ourselves and through a meaningful relationship with Jesus Christ. In Jesus, we have all we need! Instead of spending so much time thinking about what we don't have, maybe we should focus a little more on what we do have and how to use it better.

Lord, thank You for your provision. Teach me to find contentment in the pasture You have given me and make it as green as possible. I will give You all the glory. Amen.

So You're Thinking About Getting Out

"Concerning what people do: by the word of Your lips I have avoided the ways of the violent. My steps are on Your paths; my feet have not slipped."
Psalm 17:4-5

So you have doubts about coaching, about whether or not it's worth it. Sometimes the road looks too long and too tough, and you feel like quitting. You wonder if you have the determination and the energy to go through another season. Well, take an honest look at yourself. You weren't very well prepared when you started, and you made countless mistakes that cost plenty. Often you were guilty of looking for short cuts, of trying to find an easy way, when you knew very well there was no such thing.

In his book *Winning Words from Football Greats*, Larry Bielat quotes an unknown coach who said, "Over the years you've been ridiculed and treated unfairly by all kinds of people. Often your work has gone unappreciated. You've been broke. You've been tired. You've been afraid of being fired. It's tough, and it will never get any easier unless you decide to take the easy way out–which is all the way out, quitting. You may not have realized it, but from the very beginning, you were destined to be a coach. You think of all the days and all the dreams that have gone into making you what you are. Other than your family and your God, what else has ever really mattered to you? There's important work to be done, and you can do it!"

Heavenly Father, You made me and gave me special gifts to be shared with others. I want to be in Your perfect will today and every day. Help me to never give up, give in or give out. In the name of Jesus I pray. Amen.

Excellence

"Whatever you do, do it enthusiastically, as something done for the Lord and not for men, knowing that you will receive the reward of an inheritance from the Lord–You serve the Lord Christ." Colossians 3:23-24

Basketball coaching legend John Wooden once said, "Being average means you're as close to the bottom as you are to the top." When we stop and think about those words for a moment, they are profound. How often do we all settle for less than our best?

Longtime NFL coach Tony Dungy is also a man who dared to be different by demanding excellence from his players and coaches. He chose to put faith and humility at the center of his life and career. Coach Dungy believes being an excellent coach means doing everything as well as you can do it. From handling players to running practice, Dungy believes it's all about giving your best to the Lord. Coach Dungy says, "As followers of Jesus Christ, it's great to be able to show the world that, yes, we can do it the Lord's way, but we can be excellent while we do it." Our challenge is to strive for excellence in all we do. We must live out excellence not only on the field or court but also in our classrooms, churches, homes, and communities. Striving for excellence in our lives is an act of worship to an almighty God who is worthy of our best.

Heavenly Father, You have always given me Your best, and I am thankful. Push me today Lord, to give You and those You have placed in my life, my very best. It's in the name of Jesus I pray. Amen.

Strength

"Finally, be strengthened by the Lord and by His vast strength." Ephesians 6:10

As a young boy, I remember watching Paul Anderson perform incredible feats of strength during an exhibition at my high school. I was in awe of this powerful man's size and his ability to lift huge weights and large numbers of people with ease. Anderson gained worldwide attention in 1955 during an amateur weight-lifting contest in Moscow. At the age of 22, he lifted more weight on his first attempt than any of his Russian competitors. Anderson became a gold medalist at the 1956 Olympic Games in Melbourne, Australia and was known by many as the world's strongest man. He once lifted an amazing 6,270 pounds, which put him in the Guinness Book of World Records as the most weight ever raised by a human being. I also remember hearing Paul Anderson's words that day. He told the audience how God had changed his life and given him the vision to reach others for Christ. I later learned about the Paul Anderson Youth Home in Vidalia, Georgia, which has provided a Christian environment for troubled and homeless young men. Over 90% of those graduating from Anderson's miracle home have gone on to live productive lives.

In Ephesians, Paul gives us a picture of a mighty and muscular God. There is nothing more powerful than God. He created the entire universe; He flooded the earth. His Son Jesus Christ was born from a virgin's womb, and He defeated death by raising Jesus from the tomb. WOW!! Paul is reminding us to be strong and understand that all of God's power is working inside of you and me. When the troubles come or fear creeps into our minds, we must remember God has placed in each of us the power to resist and withstand anything Satan brings our way. Our challenge is to allow God to release this strength and power in us and see what a difference it makes.

Heavenly Father, Your power is above and beyond anything I can imagine. Help me remember that through the Holy Spirit, You have placed great power and strength in me. Strengthen me today to face my challenges and fears with confidence and courage. Amen.

Reaching Higher

"Love the Lord your God with all your heart, with all your soul, with all your mind, and with all your strength." Mark 12:30

Being fit is one thing; being an athlete is another. Experts say that thirty minutes of exercise at a comfortable pace four times a week will make us fit. So two hours a week of running, walking, biking, or swimming will allow an individual to maintain a basic level of fitness. It doesn't matter whether the activities are done in the morning, afternoon or evening; it just has to be scheduled and completed. Fitness can be measured and tested. It is paying attention to the minimum requirements of the body. To be an athlete requires taking training to another level. Being an athlete is not something you do for two hours a week; it is something you are. It requires twenty-four hours a day, every day. Fitness helps us see the life we should lead. Being an athlete means we have found it.

Similarly, being a Christian is one thing, but giving God everything is another. We may go to church each week, give financially, teach Sunday School and maybe even sing in the choir. We proudly collect our perfect attendance pin, convince ourselves that we put more in the offering plate than most and learn a great deal about the Bible as we prepare to teach others. How easy it is to settle for the minimum requirements of our faith. God does not want us to be spiritually fit, rather He wants us to be spiritual athletes. To become a spiritual athlete requires us to give our all twenty-four hours a day, every day. God must be the most important part of our life. We must give Him all of our heart, soul, mind and strength. We must watch what we put in our mouth, we must watch what comes out of our mouth, we must get proper rest, and we must train properly with plenty of Bible study and prayer. Being spiritually fit helps us see the life we should lead. Being a spiritual athlete means we have found it. God wants us to be Champions for Him.

Heavenly Father, take me to a new level of spiritual fitness today. Help me give You all my heart, soul, mind and strength every day. Make me a true champion for Your Kingdom. Amen.

Warriors

"They attack as warriors (attack); they scale walls as men of war (do). Each goes on his own path, and they do not change their course." Joel 2:7

When I think of warriors, usually images of Mel Gibson in *Braveheart* or Russell Crowe in *Gladiator* come to mind. In these characters, we see courage, conviction and a sense of purpose larger than life. In the world of sports, we like to see athletes compete with a warrior mentality. Former major league pitcher Nolan Ryan is remembered as a warrior. The inside of the plate was his, and he didn't mind knocking you on your backside to prove it. Mike Singletary played professional football with a desire and intensity few have duplicated, but many remember. Have you ever noticed how short many obituaries are? Everything in our life's resume gets boiled down to a few sentences. How do you want to be remembered–Hall of Fame, career victories, championships or a warrior who passionately loved God?

There is no retirement plan in our walk with God. God wants us to be warriors in our faith for as long as we have breath. Jay Bennett loves God. A successful corporate attorney and founder of the outreach ministry Christian Oil, Bennett puts it this way, "My advice is to make sure you die in battle. It's good to know what your desired outcomes and objectives are, but you never know what's going to happen in life. The key is to live intentionally, with passion, for a cause that's worth your life. And then die bloody. I plan to go down swinging; I want to die in battle." Now that's a model for life to strive for.

Heavenly Father, make me a warrior for You today. Strengthen me in the fight for things that have eternal value. Amen.

Spiritual Growth

"Now everyone who lives on milk is inexperienced with the message about righteousness, because he is an infant. But solid food is for the mature—for those whose senses have been trained to distinguish between good and evil."
Hebrews 5:13-14

One of my greatest joys as a coach is watching players mature as they move through the program. It's always exciting to see that young, skinny, uncoordinated athlete leave for the summer and return in the fall three inches taller, twenty pounds heavier and able to complete drills flawlessly. Like the ugly caterpillar that turns into a beautiful butterfly, you don't recognize them as being the same creature. It's also rewarding to witness athletes grow confident in themselves and begin to believe in the system being taught by the coaching staff. No longer content just to be on the team and stand on the sidelines, they want to lead and get into the action. The growth and maturity of these athletes are usually the direct results of consistent and persistent training of their minds and bodies.

Like athletics, spiritual growth requires consistent and persistent training as well. All too often, we witness the joy of salvation with little or no lasting change in a person's life. We see example after example of infant Christians perfectly content to continue drinking spiritual milk rather that moving toward the solid food of Christian maturity. To grow from infant Christians to mature Christians, we must learn to separate good from evil and right from wrong. Where do we go for this knowledge? Look no further than God's Word, the Bible. George Mueller, the 19th-century evangelist, had this to say, "The vigor of our spiritual lives will be in exact proportion to the place held by the Bible in our lives and our thoughts." As we grow in the Lord and put into practice what we have learned, our capacity to understand will also grow. Just like the athlete, we must always be striving to get better and refuse to stand still in our development.

Lord, give me the desire to grow in my knowledge of You and Your Word. Push me Lord, to grow in my faith and live it out each and every day. Amen.

Sacrifice

"No one takes it from Me, but I lay it down on My own. I have the right to lay it down, and I have the right to take it up again. I have received this command from My Father." John 10:18

In the world of sports, we understand the concept of sacrifice. As coaches, we sacrifice time with our own families to serve the needs of our athletes. We work countless hours with little financial reward and without complaint. We cut the grass, line the fields, maintain the equipment and deal with frustrated parents. We are often asked why we do it. The simple answer for most is that we love it! We love the game. We love to compete. We love the sounds, smells, and sheer excitement of game day. Most of all, we love our athletes. We love watching them grow and mature. We love building relationships with young men and women and seeing them achieve more than they believed they ever could. We love seeing them years later when they return as mothers and fathers and good citizens of the community to say thank you.

God, our loving Father in heaven, also understands sacrifice. He made us, and more than anything He wants to have a relationship with us. The roadblock in this desire is that God is pure, and because of our sin, we are not. Sin separates us from God. To build a bridge that allows us to reach Him, God made a sacrifice. He gave his only Son, Jesus Christ, as a sacrifice for our sins. Jesus did this voluntarily and in His Father's perfect will. Jesus endured humiliation, beatings and an agonizing death on the Cross. The question we often ask is, "Why did He do it?" The simple answer is love! John 3:16 says, "For God loved the world in this way: He gave His One and Only Son so that everyone who believes in Him will not perish but have eternal life." What a joyful day it will be when we can stand before God and have the opportunity to say, "Thank you Coach!"

Father God, thank You for loving me. Thank You for the sacrifice of Your Son, Jesus Christ, who makes it possible for me to be in relationship with You. Help me understand that love and share it with others today. Amen.

Influence

"Not that I have already reached (the goal) or am already fully mature, but I make every effort to take hold of it because I also have been taken hold of by Christ Jesus." Colossians 3:12

Influence. As coaches we have it, but the critical question each of us must answer is, how are we using it. I ran across an article recently titled, "Encouraging Coaches," which recognized several coaches who have had a lasting influence on their athletes. In one of these stories, Darryll Canida said his basketball coach, Mark Campbell, changed his life. Canida left an abusive father and Coach Campbell did his best to guide him during that difficult time. Canida said, "Coach Campbell taught me more than the game of basketball, he taught me about the game of life." Coach Campbell always made time for Canida and others on the team, even though he had a wife and four children of his own. "He took me to church, college basketball games, dinners with his family and loved me when I didn't feel lovable."

Coach Campbell has coached more than thirty years, winning state tournaments and championships, but the opportunity to be a positive role model and help steer young people in the right direction is what means the most to him. "You never know what impact you have at the time," said Campbell. Darryll Canida went on to get a master's degree and is now a middle school coach. "I am the man I am today because God put Coach Campbell in my life." Our challenge is to clothe ourselves with the compassion, kindness, humility, gentleness and patience modeled by our Lord and Savior, Jesus Christ. The Holy Spirit can use us to change lives too! Are you up to the challenge?

Heavenly Father, You have called me to coach. What a gift, and what a responsibility. Guide my steps today as I strive to be a positive influence in the lives of others. Amen.

Fathers

"The father of a righteous son will rejoice greatly, and one who fathers a wise son will delight in him." Proverbs 23:24

I am the father of two fine sons. When the youngest left home for college, my wife and I entered a new phase in our lives. The empty nest was a reality, and I would be lying if I said I didn't miss them. After years of adjusting schedules, attending ball games and constant action, it was quiet. Too quiet! I often found myself thinking about their growing up years and all the times we spent playing catch, pretending to score the game-winning touchdown and just enjoying each other's company. Where did the time go? Sometimes, in our moments of reflection, we need a good laugh, and I found it in this story from *Chicken Soup for the Sports Fan's Soul.*

"During the 1966-1967 football season, Green Bay Packer quarterback Bart Starr had a little incentive scheme going with his oldest son. For every perfect paper Bart Jr. brought home from school, his dad gave him ten cents. After one particularly rough game in which Bart Sr. felt he had performed poorly, he returned home weary and battered late at night after a long plane ride. He couldn't help feeling better when he went to his bedroom where attached to his pillow was a note that read, 'Dear Dad, I thought you played a great game. Love Bart.' Taped to the note were two dimes!" As coaches, it's easy to let our schedules squeeze our children out. One day, we will wake up to the reality that they are gone. The time goes faster than you think. Make time for your family, especially your children. Take time to play together, laugh together and tell them you love them.

Heavenly Father, thank You for the gift of being a dad. Help me remember that they are mine for a little while, but they are Yours for eternity. Help me to make my family a priority today. Amen.

Hope

"And our hope for you is firm, because we know that as you share in the sufferings, so you will share in the comfort." 2 Corinthians 1:7

There are times in our lives when we are tempted to lose hope. No one is immune. Sometimes life kicks us in the gut, and we want to scream those words coaches hate to hear, "I quit!" In times like these, it's easy just to pack it up and retreat into a world of self-pity and hopelessness. What's the use? Why bother? Does any of this matter? Even though most of us like to think we have everything under control, the truth is, we control very little. In an instant, we can find our lives turned upside down through no fault of our own. So what do we do when we don't know what to do? How do we get back on track? Zig Ziglar once said, "It's not the situation, but how we react to the situation that's important." That's good advice.

The Apostle Paul knew hard times. He was beaten, shipwrecked, and imprisoned. When those things happened, did Paul ever think about quitting? If he did, he didn't keep those thoughts very long. What did Paul know that most people don't? What gave Paul the hope to keep going? The answer is a solid trust and a firm confidence in his Lord and Savior, Jesus Christ. Paul knew he did not suffer alone. Jesus was there to provide comfort and hope for the future. He gave Paul the strength to keep moving. Jesus will do the same for us when we ask. Is your world out of control? Are you looking for hope in a difficult time? Why don't you consider a little talk with Jesus?

Lord, give me an unwavering faith in You in the midst of the storms of life, even when I don't understand why I'm going through them. Amen.

Expectations

"My eager expectation and hope is that I will not be ashamed about anything, but that now as always, with all boldness, Christ will be highly honored in my body, whether by life or by death. For me, living is Christ and dying is gain." Philippians 1:20-21

Expectations. As coaches, we run into them everywhere. Often, we fail to live up to them. We set goals each season, hoping to accomplish more than even we think is possible. There are so many expectations and so many disappointments when our goals are not met.

Dr. Joe Stowell, author, and speaker shares three areas where we often face unmet expectations: the people around us, our situations and the uncertain future ahead of us. Too often our expectations set us up for disappointments. Paul wrote about expectations while in prison. He didn't give up because of his circumstances, and he turned his prison into his pulpit. Though he didn't know what his future held, Paul made it clear his only expectation was to live for Christ and make Him the center of his life. Let me challenge you to set this single new expectation. Whoever you are with, wherever you are, regardless of the uncertainties that lie ahead, live to magnify Christ.

Heavenly Father, You know our every need. Help us look beyond the people around us, our present situation and the uncertain future. Strengthen us to live for You above all else. Amen.

Practice

"There is profit in all hard work, but endless talk leads only to poverty."
Proverbs 14:23

What does it take to be great? Is there one secret that allowed Ted Williams to become baseball's greatest hitter? What was it that allowed Hank Aaron to be the most consistent home run hitter of his era? Did Nolan Ryan, the record holder for career strikeouts, know something other pitchers didn't? Some would argue that you're either born with talent, or you're not. Others say greatness is the result of years of hard and painful work. Williams, Aaron, and Ryan were certainly gifted athletes, but let's not forget the countless hours of practice they put in during their careers. Legendary coach John Wooden is quoted as saying, "You must believe in yourself, but you can't do that if you aren't prepared." Whether it's sports, business, music or math, evidence indicates greatness isn't something we are born with but rather something that's attained through the process of deliberate practice and hard work.

The Bible indicates that God intended us to work. Work is good and should bring fulfillment and satisfaction to our lives. Without hard work, our lives would be shallow and out of balance. Hard workers are well-known by those around them. They have good reputations. We all have choices to make. We can settle for average, or we can kick it up another gear. What we make of our lives will be largely determined by our drive and determination. Will we have put in the hard work and practice when our opportunity comes? God's message to us is this—in the end, hard work pays!

Lord, You made me and You know what's best for me. Teach me the value of hard work. In Jesus' name I pray. Amen.

Heart

"Only carefully obey the command and instruction that Moses the Lord's servant gave you: to love the Lord your God, walk in His ways, keep His commands, remain faithful to Him, and serve Him with all your heart and all your soul." Joshua 22:5

How many times do we see athletes who have all the physical tools but fail to live up to their potential? Why do some athletes with everything going for them so often miss the mark while those with limited ability bring home the prize? What's the missing ingredient? Heart! Time and time again we see athletes accomplish amazing feats because they're willing to push themselves beyond the limits of others. They simply refuse to quit! The great distance runner Steve Prefontaine once said, "To give anything less than your best is to sacrifice the gift." Our hearts reveal the very core of who we are.

So, what does it mean to love Jesus Christ with all your heart? We need to look no further than the life of the apostle Paul to find the answer. Paul was a man fanatically sold out to his Lord. He worked in season and out of season. He was tireless, unstoppable and unwilling to accept defeat. There was no sacrifice too great, no price too high for him to pay. His success was the result of heart. He was bold and fearless. Paul let nothing stand in the way of his sharing the gospel. Now that's playing with heart! I pray we all will do the same.

Father, You are my strength in the difficult times. Teach me to put my trust in You and never hold back from the things You've called me to do. In Jesus' name I pray. Amen.

Responsibility

"For each person will have to carry his own load." Galatians 6:5

As coaches, we are always talking to our players about responsibility. We demand they be responsible for getting to practice on time. We expect them to be responsible for keeping up with their equipment. We warn them to be responsible for their actions off the playing field or court. Unfortunately, the world we live in doesn't help set a very good example, and this makes our job as coaches more difficult. Recent court decisions leave us scratching our heads. One jury awarded a cigarette smoker one billion dollars in damages because he developed lung cancer. A class-action suit was filed against McDonald's accusing the fast-food business of making people overweight and unhealthy. We have become a society that loves to play the blame game.

One of the things Paul is teaching us in Galatians is that all of us are accountable for certain things in life. We are expected to carry our bags. No one can do our work for us, and no one can make decisions for us. We must be responsible for paying our bills, raising our children, feeding our dog and mowing our grass. Participation in sports requires taking responsibility, and coaches must keep demanding it. Nobody gets a free ride! We all have to answer to someone. Eating too many cheeseburgers and smoking too many cigarettes may have negative consequences. Poor spiritual choices may have negative consequences too. Each of us will have to answer to God for those.

Heavenly Father, thank You for Your living Word. You have provided us with a plan to live our lives to the fullest, yet You have also given us free will. Teach me to take responsibility for my actions and make the right choices today. In Jesus' name I pray. Amen.

Team

"But our presentable parts have no need (of clothing). Instead, God has put the body together, giving greater honor to the less honorable, so that there would be no division in the body, but that the members would have the same concern for each other." 1 Corinthians 12:24-26

What more liberating experience is there than to feel whole, purposeful and in sync? We practice together, we play together, we win together and we lose together. Coaches preach that you don't just give your all to the game, you give your all to your team. Emmitt Smith's induction speech into the NFL Hall of Fame is a perfect example. With tears of gratitude, he thanked his family, former coaches, and teammates for helping him reach the pinnacle of football, but his most heartfelt thanks went to Daryl Johnston, the Dallas Cowboy fullback who cleared the path for many of Smith's great runs. "You mean the world to me," Smith told Johnston, asking him to stand up and be recognized by the crowd. "Not because we shared the same backfield but because you sacrificed so much for me. Without you, I know today would not have been possible. I love you from the bottom of my heart."

Playing as a team generates transforming power. An African-American Emmitt Smith, from Pensacola, Florida, and the University of Florida pronouncing his love and affection for a white Daryl Johnston, from Youngstown, New York, and Syracuse University. Wow! As the body of Christ, we have all been given gifts. It's important to remember that even though we are not gifted in the same way, we are linked together. What affects one member of the team affects the entire team. We need each other. We belong to each other. We affect each other. Together, we can accomplish great things.

Father, thank You for the gifts You have given me. Help me see that these gifts were not intended for my benefit, but for Your glory and in service to others. Make me a team player in the Body of Christ. Amen.

Imitators

"Therefore, be imitators of God, as dearly loved children. And walk in love."
Ephesians 5:1-2a

What players did you imitate as a kid? Growing up a huge baseball fan and watching the New York Yankees on the Game of the Week each Saturday, two of my favorite players were Mickey Mantle and Whitey Ford. Living on a farm in rural South Carolina made it difficult to find enough players for a pick-up game, so I spent a great deal of time figuring out ways to entertain myself. Many an afternoon would find me swinging at imaginary balls from my best Mickey Mantle stance or striking out another imaginary Major League hitter using my best Whitey Ford windup. Little did it matter that I was not a switch hitter like Mantle nor did I throw left-handed like Ford. What mattered was Mantle and Ford were my heroes, and I wanted to be just like them.

While most of us outgrow our childhood desire to imitate sports heroes, it's easy to fall into the trap of imitating poor behaviors and lifestyles as adults. The question we have to ask ourselves is who is the best model for our lives? The best way for us to connect with God is to imitate the life of His Son, Jesus Christ. How often do we waste precious time and effort trying to pattern ourselves after the wrong people? When we turn our lives over to Jesus, we become children of God. We take on the family resemblance and should make every effort to uphold the family name. We are to walk in love giving ourselves to others in Christian service. This is what Jesus did for us. Who is your model for life? Are they worthy of following, or do you need to make some adjustments?

Heavenly Father, You give us all we need. Thank You for the gift of Your Son, Jesus Christ. Help me model my life today after His perfect example. Amen.

It's So Boring

"Iron sharpens iron, and one man sharpens another." Proverbs 27:17

How can you run; it's so boring? As a long-time runner, I've heard that question many times. Now, I understand why running is not everyone's idea of a good time. Why run somewhere when a short ride would take you to the same place a lot quicker? What I've learned over the years is that I not only enjoy running, I need it. There's a personal satisfaction I get from having the discipline to lace up my shoes and get out for a workout. Breaking a good sweat makes me feel like I've done something. However, what I truly enjoy and need most is the social aspect of running. I like spending time with the guys as we laugh and talk about everything from sports trivia to our favorite childhood memories. We keep one another motivated and focused on the important things in life.

It's not unusual to hear the words church and boring in the same sentence too. The list of what bores people about church is endless. The service is too long, the music doesn't suit my taste, or the preacher's sermons are over my head. Being perfectly honest, I've had some of these thoughts myself on occasion. Over the years, I've learned that not only do I like church, but I need it. Yes, sometimes the service goes into overtime, but there is a blessing I would have missed had I not been there. As far as the music, I've learned to focus on the words rather than the volume or melody. I continue to be inspired by the old hymns as well as the contemporary artists of today. Pastors and their sermons come and go. However, what I enjoy most about church is the people. I like spending time with the guys not only on Sundays but through the endless opportunities I have to serve God and others in our community. Our faith and love for one another motivates me and helps me keep my life in proper focus. To me, running and church aren't boring. I need them!

Lord, thank You for Your people and Your church. Help me today to understand that iron sharpens iron and we need each other as we go through this life. Amen.

Team

"Two are better than one because they have a good reward for their efforts. For if either falls, his companion can lift him up; but pity the one who falls without another to lift him up." Ecclesiastes 4:9-10

It's not easy to build a team! As coaches, we are asked to take a group of individuals and mold them into a single unit seeking a common goal. We mix seasoned veterans with untested rookies. We fight selfishness, entitlement and lack of commitment every day. Slowly and consistently, we teach our athletes it's not about where you come from, who your parents are or what you did last year that counts. It's about attitude and effort and a willingness to be a part of something bigger than yourself. It's about coming to work every day with a desire to get better as an individual and as a team. It's about making personal sacrifices for the good of the team. It's about learning that the best teams play for each other, not with each other.

Everyone knows Solomon was a wise man, the wisest man to ever live. His words speak as loudly and clearly today as they did when he first spoke them. Solomon knew the importance of being on a team. Cooperating with others has great advantages. I believe God designed life for working together with others. God didn't create us to be alone. Some people prefer isolation, thinking they can't trust anyone. We aren't put on earth to serve ourselves, but to serve God and others. Don't isolate yourself and try to go it alone. Seek out others; be part of the team. It may be your family, it may be your coaching staff or it may be your church. They need you, and you need them.

Lord, I am humbled to be a part of Your team. Satan knows I am weak when I am alone. Bring me teammates today that will help make the work lighter and more enjoyable. Amen.

Who's the Greatest?

"Jesus told him, 'I am the way, the truth, and the life. No one comes to the Father except through Me.'" John 14:6

Who's the greatest? For generations, sports fans around the world have spent countless hours debating this question. Was Mickey Mantle better than Willie Mays? Were the undefeated Miami Dolphins the best team to ever play professional football? What about the NBA; would you take the Los Angeles Lakers or the Boston Celtics? We can argue statistics, the era in which the games were played, and share eyewitness accounts. There's no way to settle these types of questions, but as fans, they sure are fun to talk about.

As followers of Jesus Christ, others may challenge us and the words found in John 14:6. What makes Jesus the greatest? What about Mohammed, Confucius, or Buddha? First of all, Jesus is the only option which is both man and God. As the way, Jesus is our path to the Father. As the life, he joins his divine life with ours, both now and eternally. Jesus is, in truth, the only living way to the Father. Some people may argue that this way is too narrow. In reality, it is wide enough for the whole world, if the world chooses to accept it. Instead of debating how limited it sounds to have only one way, we should be saying, "Thank you, God, for providing a sure way to get to you."

Heavenly Father, thank You for sending Your Son, Jesus Christ, that I might know You and live with You for eternity. Give me the desire and the courage to share Your love with someone today. Amen.

Our Days Are Numbered

"Your eyes saw me when I was formless; all (my) days were written in Your book and planned before a single one of them began." Psalm 139:16

Life is precious! We were reminded of that in 2016, with the tragic death of Miami Marlins pitcher Jose Fernandez. So young, so full of life and a future filled with promise. At the age of twenty-four, Fernandez had accomplished so much. He posted a 38-17 record with a 2.58 ERA and averaged 11.2 strikeouts per nine innings. He won the National League Rookie of the Year Award and made two All-Star teams. He had a passion for baseball, and his smile radiated the joy of being able to play the game he loved. Players and fans loved him. He had overcome a great deal to become a Major League pitcher. Fernandez escaped Cuba with his mother and sister after three failed attempts. He learned a new language and became a United States citizen in 2015. He was back on track after rehab from Tommy John surgery. To the Latino community in South Florida, Fernandez was an inspiration and source of pride.

Life is unpredictable! With the news of Fernandez's death, we were once again reminded that we couldn't predict the future. The hard truth is we don't know how much time we have on this earth. God does not promise us tomorrow, only today. Where does that leave us? First, we need to decide how we're going to live in this world. I think Jose Fernandez had it figured out in some areas of his life. He lived with a passion for life and found joy all around him. Second, we need to decide how we're going to live in this world. Through His Son, Jesus Christ, God has promised each of us a way we can live with Him for eternity. The decision is up to us! Yes, no and maybe later are our only choices. If we chose maybe later, that time might never come. Think about it!

Heavenly Father, thank You for life. Help me live this day with passion and joy as though it's my last. Give me the boldness to share the love of Christ with someone today. Amen.

The King

"You are the king then? Pilate asked. 'You say I'm a king,' Jesus replied. 'I was born for this, and I have come into the world for this; to testify to the truth. Everyone who is of the truth listens to My voice.'" John 18:37

The man known as "The King of Golf" left us in 2016. To the golf world, Arnold Palmer was bigger than life! He burst into our living rooms with the birth of televised golf, and thousands of adoring fans became part of "Arnie's Army." Palmer not only was one of golf's greatest players, but he was also one of the game's greatest ambassadors. He connected with the masses like no other by making himself accessible. He inspired generations of players to love the game. He went on to win sixty-two titles on the PGA Tour and was also a successful businessman, philanthropist and golf course designer. People loved Arnold Palmer and admired the hard-charging way he approached the game. He was a risk taker. He won big and lost big! Palmer is quoted as saying, "the most rewarding things you do in life are often the ones that look like they can't be done." What great wisdom he spoke.

Jesus was also a king. Earthly kings of Jesus' day often quizzed Him on that title. When Pontius Pilate asked Jesus if He was a king, his response was clear. "My Kingdom is not of this world." There does not seem to be any doubt in Pilate's mind that Jesus was speaking the truth. It's also doubtful that Pilate believed Jesus stood before him guilty of committing a crime. Pilate, however, like so many others, made a grave mistake. While recognizing the truth, he chose to reject it. To most, Jesus did not look like a king, and He didn't act like any king they had ever seen. How could a man from Nazareth, the son of a carpenter, be the long-awaited Messiah? For centuries, this man called Jesus has been doing what others said couldn't be done. He transforms lives, He softens hearts and He makes the impossible possible. When we turn our lives over to Him and become part of God's Army, we will never be the same.

Heavenly Father, thank You for Your Son Jesus. Help me do the impossible today through Your strength and promises. Amen.

In the Trenches

"It must not be like that among you. On the contrary, whoever wants to become great among you must be your servant, and whomever wants to be first among you must be your slave; just as the Son of Man did not come to be served, but to serve, and to give His life–a ransom for many." Matthew 20:26-28

There is little mystery why the lineman mentality is part of my DNA. The little hand-written sign in my dad's office flashed like a neon sign when I walked in each day. It read, "Don't worry about the credit, just get the job done!" You just have to love linemen. Coaches know football games are won and lost in the trenches; yet to the average fan, linemen are just over-sized guys who get in the way of the running backs and receivers. Merlin Olson, a Hall of Fame NFL lineman, once said, "Football linemen are motivated by a more complicated self-determined series of factors than the simple fear of humiliation in the public gaze, which is the emotion that galvanizes the back and receivers." From that very statement, you can tell linemen are intelligent. They are also tenacious, relentless and stubborn. With little visible reward or public recognition, they serve their team.

A little of the lineman mentality would serve us well in our faith journey as well. Like Jesus' disciples, we often spend too much time and effort trying to be the greatest. How often are we like the running back or receiver who enters the end zone, thrusts the ball in the air, and breaks into his version of a touchdown celebration? Look at me; look what I did for Jesus! Christ said things are different in His Kingdom; greatness is defined by service. The life of Jesus can be summed up in two words–serve and give. A humble King was born in a manger and died on a cross for you and me. Are we worried about looking good and receiving the credit or just getting the job done? Are we tenacious, relentless and stubborn when it comes to serving and sharing our love of Jesus Christ with others?

Jesus, this serving thing is hard! I struggle daily with the me first mentality. I confess my selfishness. Help me see through Your eyes the ways I can serve my team. I want to be consumed to serve. Amen.

Punting Into the Wind

"Now if any of you lacks wisdom, he should ask God, who gives to all generously and without criticizing, and it will be given to him. But let him ask in faith without doubting. For the doubter is like the surging sea, driven and tossed by the wind." James 1:5-6

My faith was wavering. As I watched my unpredictable punter jog onto the field, doubt washed over me with every step. I never knew what to expect; it might go forty yards in a tight spiral, or it could be a ten-yard shank off the side of his foot. Every kick was an unpredictable adventure. It was late in the game, and field position was critical as my team lined up in punt formation. As the punter waited for the snap from center, the unexpected happened. The gentle breeze that had been blowing all night suddenly transformed into a very stiff wind. My punter handled the snap cleanly, took two steps and kicked the ball high into the air. At that point, the play seemed to move in slow-motion. Everyone watched as a gust of wind caught the ball mid-flight and pushed it backward! When the ball finally came to rest, and the official blew his whistle, we realized we had witnessed an unbelievable negative ten-yard punt. My doubts had been confirmed, and the untimely wind had managed to make a bad situation worse.

Too often, we approach God with the same doubt as I did my punter. Sometimes we're optimistic, and sometimes we're pessimistic. We know God can do it, but the results don't always turn out as we want. We know God cares about us and loves us, but why don't we always get a positive result? When doubt creeps into our faith, we often get tossed around and pushed backward like that wind-blown punt. Our doubt does not honor God, and chances are slim that wisdom and insight will come from our wishy-washy belief. Want better results? Take a firm stand the next time you pray; talk to God with complete faith and remember no doubting allowed!

Heavenly Father, protect me from the winds of doubt. Teach me to be strong in my faith and trust You completely in all things. Amen.

Between a Rock and a Hard Place

"As Pharaoh approached, the Israelites looked up and saw the Egyptians coming after them. Then the Israelites were terrified and cried out to the Lord for help." Exodus 14:10

As coaches, it's not unusual to find ourselves in tight spots during competition. How we respond to those situations can reveal a great deal about our commitment and faith in what we are trying to accomplish. Buffalo Bills coach, Marv Levy, found himself in one of those tight spots in a 1992 NFL contest with the Houston Oilers. Trailing 35-3 in the third quarter, it looked hopeless for the Bills, who were playing without their regular quarterback and escape artist, Jim Kelly. It was then that backup quarterback Frank Reich led an incredible comeback. Reich threw four touchdown passes–the last three to Andre Reed–to propel Buffalo into a 35-35 tie at the end of regulation. The game went into overtime, and Steve Christie's 32-yard field goal sealed the unlikely victory. The Buffalo Bills found themselves between a rock and a hard place yet kept the faith in the game plan and the abilities of the team.

Moses found himself between a rock and a hard place as he fled the chariots of the great Pharaoh. Escape seemed impossible for the two million Israelites trapped by the Red Sea. When they looked up and saw the Egyptian army coming toward them, they were terrified and cried out to the Lord. They were also quick to complain to Moses, saying it would have been better to serve the Egyptians than to die in the wilderness. It's apparent the Israelites had lost hope in the game plan and the abilities of the team. Moses told them to hold still, and what came next was one of the greatest miracles in all history. As Moses raised his staff, God parted the Red Sea, and the Israelites walked on dry land to the other side. What a comeback! How exciting is it to know the faith that opened the Red Sea also enables us to do the impossible, when we are moving forward in the will of God.

Heavenly Father, guide me in Your perfect plan today. Thank You for being my rock when I encounter the hard places. Amen.

Friendship

"A friend loves at all times, and a brother is born for a difficult time." Proverbs 17:17

The value of true friendship is priceless. At the 1936 Berlin Olympic Games, Japanese pole vaulters Shuhei Nishida and Sueo Oe tied for second place. The teammates were offered the opportunity to have a jump-off for the silver medal, but the two friends declined out of mutual respect for one another. For Olympic records, Oe agreed to the bronze medal while Nishida took the silver. Upon their return to Japan, the teammates came up with a different solution. The pair had a jeweler cut their medals in half and fuse them back together, creating half-silver, half-bronze awards. The Medals of Friendship, as they're known in Japan, are lasting symbols of friendship and teamwork.

Proverbs 17:17 reminds us that a true friend loves in adversity as well as in times of prosperity. One of the greatest possessions we can have is a friend who will stand by our side when we need them the most. It's not hard to find the Lord Jesus in this verse. Well-known hymn writer Johnson Oatman once said, "There's not an hour that He is not near us, no not one! No, not one! No night so dark, but His love can cheer us, no not one! No, not one!" Do you have a friend like that? Are you a friend like that?

Heavenly Father, thank You for giving me friends who walk with me through the good times and the bad. Help me understand that it is not enough to just have good friends, but I must also be a great friend. Most of all Lord, I thank You for Your promise to always be near me! Amen.

Goals

"I pursue as my goal the prize promised by God's heavenly call in Christ Jesus." Philippians 3:14

As coaches, we go into every season with goals. There's always a prize we're chasing. It could be a state championship or maybe just to win more games than we did last season. Regardless of the goal, we know it will take hard work and relentless pursuit to achieve them. During the 2004 Olympics in Athens, Greece, American sharpshooter Matt Emmons had all but won the gold medal. He was far ahead of his competition in the 50-meter rife competition, and only a disaster could keep him from the greatest victory of his life. He looked through the scope, squeezed the trigger and watched as his round hit the bulls-eye. Olympic gold! But wait; what were the judges talking about? It was then Emmons realized he had fired on the wrong target! The mistake caused him to fall from first place to eighth place and out of the running for a medal. Emmons's tragic error reminds us that while we should have a target to aim for in life, it must be the right one!

The Apostle Paul knew the importance of setting goals. Paul wrote his letter to the Philippians while handcuffed to a guard in a dark and filthy prison. Even in the worst of circumstances, Paul kept his faith and continued to pursue heavenly goals. Regardless of Paul's suffering, he longed for Jesus Christ. This gave him the hope and motivation to keep pressing on. As God's people, it's important we set goals that are consistent with God's will for our lives and then press on in the direction of those goals. Living a life that is pleasing to God should be our primary goal. Paul had it tough; things didn't always go his way. However, God gave him His strength when he needed it. He will do the same for you.

Heavenly Father, help me keep my eyes on the right targets today. Give me Your strength to handle the tough times when they come. Keep me in Your perfect will. Amen.

Counting the Cost

"For which of you, wanting to build a tower, doesn't first sit down and calculate the cost to see if he has enough to complete it?" Luke 14:28

Everything costs something! How many times have we heard our athletes say something like, "Coach, I wish I had taken my grades more seriously," or "If I had only worked harder in the weight room, I might have been able to play in college." Unfortunately, it's also common to hear coaches say that the profession cost them their marriage and their family. Life is a tough teacher! The cost of having the chance to play on the next level often comes down to paying the price in the classroom and the weight room. The cost of maintaining a healthy family life and marriage is finding a way to balance work and home. All too often, we fail to count the cost of achieving our goals. We glamorize the end result without realizing the day-to-day struggle involved. We are great at starting off in a blaze, only to fizzle out as time goes by. A half-hearted effort seldom produces success and usually is the source of great regret.

Jesus reminds us that there is also a cost in following Him. He compared the Christian life to building a tower. The first thing a logical builder would do is to estimate the cost of construction. If there are not enough resources to complete the project, don't start it. How foolish would it look if we only laid the foundation and then stopped! Jesus uses this illustration to drive home a very important message. If we want to follow Jesus, we had better think long about the cost of abandoning our life to live a life for Him. It's a daily battle, and a half-hearted effort won't get it done.

Heavenly Father, teach me that everything has a cost. Give me wisdom to weigh that cost before committing to anything. Strengthen me to give my all in serving You and those You put in my life today. Amen.

Giving Thanks

"Rejoice always! Pray constantly. Give thanks in everything, for this is God's will for you in Jesus Christ." 1 Thessalonians 5:16-18

Life comes at us fast! As coaches, we wear many hats and have more on our to-do lists than we have time to accomplish. We interact with administrators, teachers, student/athletes, parents, spouses and our children on a daily basis. Though we have some voice over who makes the team, schedules and game day decisions, many aspects of our job are beyond our control. Injuries, suspensions, illness, and firings are not things we decide. Our faith is always stronger when things are going well. Where do we put Christ when the tough times come? Where do we find peace and comfort when the world turns on us?

As coaches, we want our players and fans to have faith in our program. We want them to stick with us not only during the good times but also through the hard times. God expects the same from us. How can we develop an attitude that will take us through the difficult times? God's Word tells us to "rejoice always, pray constantly and to give thanks in all things." That's advice we can always count on.

Heavenly Father, may I rejoice in my circumstances with the knowledge that You are always with me. May I understand You are only a prayer away regardless of my situation. Give me a heart of thanksgiving today and every day. Amen.

Coachable

"Apply yourself to instruction and listen to words of knowledge." Proverbs 23:12

A great deal of our time as coaches is spent giving instruction. Day after day we teach, reinforce and test our athletes in the skills of the sport. We give chalk talks, run drills and simulate game situations to prepare our team for competition. We expect our athletes to listen, learn and demonstrate the instructions we give them. While the ability to listen is important, I have learned that coachable athletes tend to be more successful. The coachable athlete doesn't just listen, they seek knowledge. They want to get better and are open to any and all instruction that will help them achieve their goals.

Let's take a moment to look in the mirror. How coachable are you? In the arena of athletics and life, the people most likely to gain knowledge are those who are willing to listen. Those who take success to a higher level seek knowledge. They believe paying attention to what others have to say is a sign of strength, not weakness. People who are eager to listen continue to learn and grow throughout their lives. If we refuse to become set in our ways, we can always expand the limits of our knowledge. Ask God to make you more coachable—not only in your profession but also in your family life and your relationship with Jesus Christ.

Lord, help me be a better listener today. Help me seek out others who can make me a better coach and person. May I be a seeker of Your wisdom and knowledge today and every day. Amen.

Feeding the Hungry

"Then Jesus said, 'Have the people sit down.' There was plenty of grass in that place, so they sat down. The men numbered about 5,000. Then Jesus took the loaves, and after giving thanks He distributed them to those who were seated—so also with the fish, as much as they wanted." John 6:10-11

How much is enough? As coaches, we're in a constant search for more. We never have enough pitching, we need more depth on the defensive line or we would match up better if we had more height. Most coaches don't have the luxury of picking their teams; we must work with the talent we have. Even if we recruit our teams, seldom do we get everyone we want. Too often, we tend to focus on what we don't have rather than on what we do have. That's a shame because all too often we miss an incredible blessing. As we make excuses, our athletes hunger for what we have to offer.

In John 6, Jesus gives us an incredible example of doing much with little as he feeds the 5,000 with a couple of fish and five loaves of bread. The boy shows up with everything he has and offers it to Jesus with great expectation. Jesus replies as only He can and says, "That's enough!" As His skeptical disciples look on, Jesus not only feeds the 5,000, He has twelve baskets left over. He fed them all! What do you have to offer? Jesus wants us to know that what we have is important. It might not be much, but when we give it to the Master Coach, He can perform miracles. A little in the hands of God can be transformed into something beyond our imagination. The world is hungry for His Word and His Truth. Are you willing to give it all to Jesus?

Heavenly Father, thank You for those who believe. Thank You for taking what I have and showing me that in Your hands, it's enough. Help me to always feed the hungry, in both body and spirit. Amen.

Titles

"She will give birth to a son, and you are to name Him Jesus, because He will save His people from their sins." Matthew 1:21

Titles often command great respect. The President of the United States is considered to be the most powerful person in the world. Many nations around the world are ruled by kings and queens. We put our health in the hands of doctors and turn to our pastors for spiritual guidance. What about coaches? Do we fully understand and appreciate the level of respect that goes with the title of coach? My guess is no!

In the book of Matthew, we are told of an amazing birth to come. Mary is to have a son, and Joseph is instructed to name him Jesus. He is called King, Lamb of God, and Prince of Peace to name just a few. Do we fully understand and appreciate the meaning of these titles? Again, my guess is no! As coaches, we are given a high calling. We are responsible for helping shape the lives of the athletes we serve. Coaches can change lives. God is also in the business of changing lives. To save us from a life of sin, He came to earth as a baby. That baby, Jesus, took our sins to the cross so we can spend eternity in Heaven with God, our Heavenly Father. Remember, Jesus is our Savior and our only hope. Remember, many of our athletes are looking to us for a little hope too.

Heavenly Father, thank You for the miracle of Your Son. You sent Jesus to change lives for eternity. Use me today so I too can change the lives of those You have called me to serve. Amen.

Seeing the Big Picture

"So if you have been raised with the Messiah, seek what is above, where the Messiah is, seated at the right hand of God. Set your minds on what is above, not on what is on the earth." Colossians 3:1-2

Have you ever lost perspective? Sometimes, we are so close to the action we can't see the bigger picture. Coaches, athletes, and spectators participating in a sporting event all have a limited perspective. They only experience the sights and sounds inside the stadium itself. Their eyes are glued to the field. They are caught up in the action taking place right in front of them. When the Goodyear Blimp appeared on the sports scene, television audiences were introduced to a different perspective. Viewers were allowed to see things in another dimension. From thousands of feet in the air, not only could the field be seen but also the entire stadium filled with fans. The view expanded to include the entire city surrounding the stadium. The game taking place on the field could easily become insignificant as viewers took in the panoramic view from above.

As Christ followers, we are easily consumed with what is going on around us. World events, jobs, and providing for and protecting our families dominate our thoughts. Our eyes tend to focus on what is taking place right in front of us. The Apostle Paul warns us not to get caught up in a worldly perspective. "Look up," he shouts. Be alert to what is going on around Christ; that's where the action is. We are encouraged to look at things from a heavenly perspective. We are called to live as citizens of Heaven even though our feet are walking on this earth. We are challenged to say goodbye to our former way of life and go after the life modeled by Jesus. We are promised that the new perspective will be breathtaking!

Lord, it's so easy for me to lose perspective. I struggle to see the bigger picture because I get bogged down with my limited view. Help me today to see the things You see. Amen.

Driving the Bus

"The one who trusts in himself is a fool, but one who walks in wisdom will be safe." Proverbs 28:26

Have you ever thought too highly of yourself? I was guilty of falling into that trap as a young coach working with a very successful high school program. As head coach of the junior varsity football team, I was proud of the fact we were winning and gave much of the credit for our success to my masterful coaching. Looking back, I see how foolish I was. The reality of the situation was that I had talented athletes who could play. I can laugh about this now, but I honestly believe the most important role I had was to successfully drive the team to the game and open the bus door. The program and the athletes were the reasons for success, not an immature coach with an overly inflated ego.

Putting too much trust in our abilities is a recipe for disaster. I have heard it said that ego has a huge appetite, but the more we feed it, the hungrier it gets. The Bible teaches that everything we have is a gift from God. He desires that we use these gifts to serve others and to bring Him glory. Wisdom also comes from God, and we must be careful not to take ourselves too seriously. When we start thinking it's all about us, we can expect an attitude adjustment is in our future. It's a wise person who spends more time looking up to God than staring at themselves in the mirror.

Heavenly Father, give me the wisdom to see things through Your eyes. Help me today, Lord, to comprehend the little me and the big You. Teach me to simply drive the bus, open the doors and let You do the rest. Amen.

Outward Appearance

"But the Lord said to Samuel, 'Do not look at his appearance or his stature, because I have rejected him. Man does not see what the Lord sees, for man sees what is visible, but the Lord sees the heart.'" 1 Samuel 16:7

As coaches, we are always evaluating. He's too small…too short… can't play…will never survive! Players sometimes don't fit our standard and are overlooked for playing time or even making the team. In an age when quarterbacks are 6'4" and defensive linemen weigh 300 pounds, we often thumb our noses at players we don't think can get the job done. One of the best players on the field in the 2015 and 2016 National Championship games was an undersized wide receiver who played like an All-American. Clemson University's Hunter Renfrow is listed as 5-foot-11, but is probably closer to 5-foot-9. To reach his official weight of 180, one of the Tiger's linemen would need to have his foot on the scale. As a freshman walk-on, Renfrow barely lifted 135 pounds, but his teammates quickly learned that the little guy could play! Renfrow caught the winning touchdown pass with one second remaining in Clemson's 35-31 victory over Alabama in the 2016 National Championship game. Following the game, an NFL scout said, "Playing as he did twice against Alabama, against a defense full of guys who will be playing at this level and consistently getting open and making plays, you better believe he has grabbed our attention."

God saw something special in a young boy that no one else could see. David grabbed His attention! He didn't look like a king! David was the youngest of Jesse's sons and only a shepherd. His outward appearance didn't make David a likely candidate for God's Army. The difference was his heart for the Lord. Many only saw a young shepherd boy, but God saw a man after His own heart. God is always looking for people He can use to do His work. To God, our heart condition is much more important than our physical condition. Coaches love athletes with heart, and so does God.

Heavenly Father, help me cast aside my limitations. Help me see great things can be accomplished when I seek to do them for Your honor and glory. Amen.

Criticism

"A city is built up by the blessing of the upright, but it is torn down by the mouth of the wicked." Proverbs 11:11

If you have been coaching very long, you have probably developed a thick skin. It's not easy being in the line of fire for criticism that can come from any direction. Administrators, fans, fellow coaches and players all have their own expectations of the job we should be doing. It's easy for us to question ourselves and crumble under the attack. David Roper, in his book *A Burden Shared*, says "there are four truths about criticism: (1) it always comes when we need it the least; (2) it often comes when we least deserve it; (3) it usually comes from people who are the least qualified to give it; and (4) it frequently comes in a form that is the least helpful to us."

I don't know what criticisms you face today, but I would like to offer the following suggestions for dealing with them. First, stay calm and take your case to the Lord in prayer. Don't quit, and don't stop. Count on the Lord to give you the strength and courage to face the storm. Find a brother or sister in Christ who can provide consistent encouragement. Seek relief and peace in His Word. And finally, know you are never alone. Remember every person you meet today is either a demolition site or a construction opportunity. Your words make a difference. Will they be weapons for destruction or tools for construction?

Lord, help me choose my words carefully today. Help me build others up rather than tear them down. Amen.

Obedience

"However, I did give them this command: Obey Me, and then I will be your God and you will be My people. You must walk in every way I command you so that it may go well with you." Jeremiah 7:23

Successful coaches must have players who listen and are obedient. I'll never forget the time I was coaching my son's T-ball team. Hunter was only four years old, but he was allowed to play with our five and six-year-old group. Hunter was enthusiastic but had little experience playing the game. When he hit the ball, his coaches were always very encouraging. "Run Hunter, run!" To help Hunter know exactly where to run, our first base coach decided to be more specific, "Run to me Hunter; run to me!" In our first game of the season, Hunter was obedient. He made contact with the ball, ran straight to the first base coach's box, and hugged his coach. He was promptly tagged out. We all had a good laugh because Hunter had done exactly as he was instructed.

God calls his believers to be obedient too. Obedience to God allows us to grow in our relationship with Him as we mature in our faith. God set up a system of sacrifices to encourage the Israelites to joyfully obey Him. God required the people to make these sacrifices, not to please Him but to help them see their sin and develop a genuine desire to live for Him. They had faithfully been making the sacrifices, but they had forgotten the reason they were offering them, and therefore they disobeyed God. Jeremiah reminded the people that unless they were prepared to obey God in all areas of life, simply performing the religious rituals were meaningless. God is encouraging you today as He says, "Run to me Coach, and all will be well!"

Heavenly Father, You are a God worthy of my trust. Help me be obedient today in all You call me to do. Teach me to rely on You alone and not my own desires. Amen.

Genuine Imitation

"The one who conceals his sins will not prosper, but whoever confesses and renounces them will find mercy." Proverbs 28:13

Growing up, I remember getting a new basketball for my birthday one year. It was just what I wanted. After taking it out of the box, I took my time just looking at it. It felt good in my hands, and it had that awesome new smell. As I continued to inspect the latest addition to my sporting goods collection, I noticed these words stamped on the ball, Genuine Imitation Leather. Genuine Imitation is what we call an oxymoron, a figure of speech that combines contradictory terms. You know, like jumbo shrimp and awfully good. Words that when put together, kind of mess with your brain. Now let's look at the word genuine. A dictionary would define genuine as authentic or real. An imitation, of course, is a copy or a fake of the real thing. So the question that must be asked is, how can you have a real-fake?

Isn't it amazing how easy it is to be a genuine imitation or a real fake in our faith? I'm the master of hiding things that would put me in a negative light. While I take no delight in doing this, I know I'm only one member of a very large club. We're all pretty good at it! Now let's be honest with ourselves; our sin will find us out. God will find a way to bring it to the surface and into the light. He always does. As a dad, I often told my sons as they left the house to make good choices, but sometimes they didn't. There were times they confessed their poor choices to me and other times they didn't. Life was always a little smoother in our house when things were out in the open rather than being hidden in the dark. That's also the way it works in our relationship with God, our Father. There are no blessings for us when we try to hide our sins from God. However, when we confess them to Him not only are they forgiven, but they are also forgotten. God wants to bless us. Is there something you are hiding today? Give it to God.

Heavenly Father, thank You for being a God of mercy. Forgive me for the times I try to hide things from You. Guide me today to make my life genuine and real. Amen.

175

A Change of Plans

"For I know the plans I have for you–(this is) the Lord's declaration–plans for (your) welfare, not for disaster, to give you a future and a hope." Jeremiah 29:11

Every good coach competes with a firm game plan in place. Through countless hours of film study, we have an idea of an opponent's tendencies, strengths, and weaknesses. Practice sessions are structured to help players recognize these tendencies and prepare for the expected. However, rarely do things go the way we plan or expect. In football, we have fumbles and interceptions. In basketball, we see bad passes go out of bounds and missed free throws. In baseball, errors are often the difference between winning and losing. And who hasn't played a round of golf and hit one into the woods or a sand trap? It's not how we respond to the expected that challenges us but how we deal with the unexpected. Sports and life are all about making adjustments and moving forward.

Jeremiah gives us some sound coaching advice. God promises He has plans for us. It's interesting that God says plans, not plan. This would imply He not only has a plan but at least one backup. Could it be that God has a Plan A, but when we mess up, He also has a Plan B? I would suspect most of us are not living the Plan A God intended. Some of us are much farther down the alphabet than we would prefer. That realization can be depressing, and it's easy to convince ourselves that we have failed God too many times. Facing the unexpected can be scary and even paralyzing. Jeremiah assures us that God not only has His plans but that those plans give us hope and future. It doesn't matter if it's Plan A or Plan Z, God does not give up on us. God has more than one way to get there; we just have to keep doing our part. Never doubt He is working to fulfill those plans.

Father, You are the God of the unexpected! You parted the Red Sea, You changed Saul's heart on the road to Damascus, and You brought a Savior into the world as a baby. Thank You for Your promise of hope and a future through Your plans. Thank You for not giving up on me. Amen.

You Are What You Think

"Finally brothers, whatever is true, whatever is honorable, whatever is just, whatever is pure, whatever is lovely, whatever is commendable–if there is any moral excellence and if there is any praise–dwell on these things." Philippians 4:8

Coaches are very busy people! Often we find ourselves jumping from one thing to the next in a frantic attempt to keep up. It's very easy to find ourselves reacting to everything around us rather than taking the time to think things through. In his book *Who Wants to Be a Champion?* Pat Williams states that "champions must find time to think." According to Williams, "Champions think positive thoughts, correct thoughts, big thoughts, pure thoughts and unique thoughts."

The Bible teaches us that we can control what we think. God's Word says we can't have evil thoughts and thoughts about the Lord Jesus at the same time. The Apostle Paul gives us some advice regarding our thought life. Paul says "followers of Jesus Christ think about everything that is true, noble, just, pure, lovely, of good report, virtuous and praiseworthy." We are all called to think! A pure thought life is key for spiritual, emotional, mental and physical health. Our challenge is to look at ourselves honestly. Do you need to get rid of any stinking thinking? You can start today.

Heavenly Father, guide my thoughts today. Help me think through each decision wisely and keep my focus on You. Amen.

A Helping Hand

"Iron sharpens iron, and one man sharpens another." Proverbs 27:17

In his research, Dr. Jeff Duke of 3Dimensional Coaching Institute, has found the average survival rate of a coach is just 3.2 years. In a time when quality coaches are needed more than ever, why are they leaving the profession so quickly? The answers are not hard to find. All coaches, and especially new coaches, are confronted with tremendous challenges: demand on personal time and family, stress and burnout, balancing the classroom with coaching, parent and community relations, player attitudes and discipline, budget constraints and job security are at the top of the list. As these issues force good men and women to leave careers, they prepared for and love, an even bigger question must be asked. Is there anything that can be done to keep them? I believe there is!

Every coach I know could use some encouragement and guidance on a regular basis. The Bible tells us we need a friend, and we also need to be a friend. What if, as coaches, we took Proverbs 27:17 to another level and were intentional about supporting one another? What could happen when two coaching friends brought their ideas together and helped one another in dealing with and overcoming the many coaching challenges we encounter every day? What if two coaches cared enough to challenge each other without involving egos in the discussion? For the seasoned coach, is there a young coach you could reach out to and build a relationship with? For the rookie coach, is there a veteran coach you could reach out to for guidance in your personal and professional growth? Coaching is truly a calling, and I don't believe we were created to walk the journey alone. What are you waiting for; give another coach a helping hand.

Heavenly Father, thank You for the wisdom of Your Word. Remove our sinful desire to make our own way as we face the challenges today will bring. Bring people into our lives who will guide us and encourage us. Help us to be that kind of person for someone else today. Amen.

The Big Head

"In all his scheming, the wicked arrogantly thinks: There is no accountability, (since) God does not exist." Psalm 10:4

Have you ever had a time in your coaching career when you began to think too highly of yourself? Maybe you won the big game against your bitter rival or completed an undefeated season. Maybe you received that coveted Coach of the Year award given by the local media. It's so easy to fall in love with ourselves and our accomplishments. Usually, something or someone brings us back to earth from our prideful journey. Speedy Morris, former men's basketball coach at La Salle University, tells this story. "When I first got the job at La Salle, the phone rang, and my wife told me it was Sports Illustrated. I cut myself shaving and fell down the steps in my rush to get to the phone. When I got there, a voice on the other end said, 'For just seventy-five cents an issue'…."

Without question, there is a little Speedy Morris in each of us. God's Word is full of men and women who suffered greatly due to misplaced pride. We must be on guard and remind ourselves daily that He is the giver of all things good. Our challenge is to humble ourselves before God every day. We must always give Him the praise He deserves and pray He will use us in mighty ways for His glory.

Heavenly Father, remind me today that You are always big, and I am always small. Keep me humble and help me keep my eyes on You. Amen.

A Little Extra

"And if anyone forces you to go one mile, go with him two." Matthew 5:41

Each year as basketball's March Madness begins, I'm reminded of how often games are decided by the ability to execute the fundamentals of the game. Making clutch free throws, getting the ball inbounds against a pressing defense and boxing out for a rebound can mean the difference in winning and losing. Teams that do the little things move on, and the teams that don't go home. Successful coaches and athletes spend hours of practice time to become fundamentally sound. Coaches then spend extra time watching the video, and athletes shoot hundreds of free throws in an empty gym long after practice is over. As coaches and players, we can be successful by meeting the requirements, but to be a champion we have to go the extra mile.

According to Roman law, a soldier could require a non-citizen to carry his equipment for one mile. The person had to stop what he was doing and carry the soldier's armor, shield, and food, or face punishment and sometimes death. Jesus uses this illustration to teach a difficult lesson. He encourages his followers to do what is asked, and then do more! When we think we have done enough, Jesus tells us to keep going. As coaches, we don't question the importance of going the extra mile in our sport, but how about in our personal lives? Are we going the extra mile in our marriages, in maintaining our health, in our prayer life, and studying God's Word? Are we making the extra effort to spend time with the ones we love the most? Jesus went the extra mile for us, and He is asking that we live that way too. Jesus doesn't want us to settle for average. He encourages us to give a little extra and then see how He blesses our efforts.

Heavenly Father, You are an above and beyond God! Push me today Lord to go the second mile in all I do. Strengthen me to give just a little extra in service to You and to others. Amen.

True Leadership

"Do nothing out of rivalry or conceit, but in humility consider others as more important than yourselves. Everyone should look out not only for his own interests, but also for the interests of others. Make your own attitude that of Christ Jesus." Philippians 2:3-5

John Wooden was one of the greatest coaches of all time. Nicknamed The Wizard of Westwood, his UCLA teams won ten national championships in a twelve-year span, including seven in a row. Wooden was named National Coach of the Year six times. He was inducted into the Basketball Hall of Fame as both a player and a coach and was the first person to ever have this distinction. Each year, as the NCAA Basketball Tournament plays out, I think about Coach Wooden and the impact he had on so many lives. His values and character live on through the lives of those he influenced. The principles that shaped his life are timeless and apply to coaches and athletes, regardless of sport or level of competition. Wooden believed in treating people with respect. He believed in making friends before you needed them. Wooden wanted his team members to know they were working with him and not for him. And most of all, he believed that love is the greatest word in our language.

In what ways do you model Christ's service to others on your team, your family, and your community? Do you believe in the same values Coach Wooden believed in? Are you giving your time, talents and treasures to others? Are you living a life worth modeling? If not, are you willing to do what it takes to make some changes in your life?

Heavenly Father, teach me to serve as Your Son Jesus served. Teach me Lord, that it's not about me. Help me today to have a Christ-like attitude in all I do. Amen.

Leaving a Legacy

"I am able to do all things through Him who strengthens me." Philippians 4:13

Kay Yow left a legacy! The legendary women's basketball coach at North Carolina State won 737 games, coached North Carolina State to four Atlantic Coast Conference tournament championships, and had 20 appearances in the NCAA tournament and one Final Four in 1998. She coached the United States women's team to gold medals at the 1988 Seoul Olympics, the 1986 World Championships, and the 1986 Goodwill Games. In 2000, Yow was named the Division I Women's Basketball Coach of the Year and was inducted into the Naismith Hall of Fame in 2002. The numbers and awards, however, are not the legacy of Kay Yow.

Her three-time battle with breast cancer and how she faced her trials head-on will be what is remembered by those whose lives she touched. Yow refused to feel sorry for herself. "I don't think, why me? I don't think anything; it's life. As you go through life, it's inevitable that you're going to face tough times." Her players say she taught them more than basketball skills. She touched them with her presence. Despite her failing health, Yow was selfless, never missing a day. What was the source of Kay Yow's strength? When asked by a player how she was doing, she responded, "I am great because God allowed me to wake up this morning. Nothing is going to happen today that God and I can't handle!" A humble warrior who cared about people lived with passion and made a difference in the lives of others is how Coach Yow will be remembered. Now that's a legacy worth leaving behind!

Heavenly Father, I want to be a warrior for You today. Keep me humble, give me a passion for life and give me the strength to make a difference in the lives of others. Amen.

Footwork

As coaches, we spend hours helping our athletes develop correct footwork. We realize any skill, regardless of how simple it seems, has to be taught and practiced on a consistent basis. Wise coaches know that teaching correct footwork can be the difference between winning and losing. Having our athletes practice correct footwork is an important part of developing them into complete players. Typically, the athletes who can move effectively on the field or court experience greater success.

Footwork is important in our Christian walk as well. God plans and arranges the steps of those who live in fellowship with Him. He is always there to lift us up when we are striving to please Him. Does this make us immune to trials and hardship? No! What it does mean, however, is that God will never let us be consumed by our difficulties. He holds us in His hand. All too often we get caught up in our fancy footwork rather than walking the pathway God has laid out. It is up to us to learn the footwork techniques the Master Coach is teaching and practicing them on a consistent basis.

Lord Jesus, guide my steps today. Keep me on the path You would have me to walk. Amen.

Character

"All the ways of a man seem right to him, but the Lord evaluates the motives."
Proverbs 21:2

How many times have we heard a coach say, "Sports build character?" In his book, *Inside/Out Coaching,* Joe Ehrmann calls this one of the great myths in America. "Most of us would probably agree that they can and should, but all too often the experience falls short of what it could be." Ehrmann goes on to say, "Sports don't build character unless a coach possesses character and intentionally teaches it." Now there's something to chew on for a while. I got into coaching because I loved to compete and wanted to stay close to the game, but I also became a coach because I loved, admired and looked up to the men and women who made it a positive experience for me. They encouraged me, put my needs above their own and cared about me as a person more than they did as an athlete. They were positive examples of character because they lived it. Sports were good for me because my coaches were good for me. Because character was important to them, it became important to me.

Today's verse forces us to ask some tough questions. Are we in it for ourselves or for the athletes we are called to serve? Why do we do what we do? Our outward appearance can deceive others, and we can even fool ourselves for a while, but God knows our motives. God knows our heart! In the end, it's not what the world thinks of us but what God will say to us when we stand before Him. We should all strive to hear those words, "Well done, good and faithful servant."

Father, thank You for putting men and women in my life who have modeled the true meaning of character. Make me intentional in being a person of character to those whom I influence. Amen.

New Beginnings

"Brothers, I do not consider myself to have taken hold of it. But one thing I do: forgetting what is behind and reaching forward to what is ahead, I pursue as my goal the prize promised by God's heavenly call in Jesus Christ. Philippians 3:13-14

There is something magical about the beginning of a new season of Major League baseball. Stadiums are packed with enthusiastic fans, and memories of days gone by are relived as former greats throw out the first pitch. Everyone puts aside the disappointments of the previous season, replacing them with endless possibilities of what the new season will bring. New beginnings and a fresh start! As an Atlanta Braves fan, this translates into pumped up fans cheering wildly as Henry Aaron throws a soft toss to Bobby Cox at home plate and the umpire yells, "Play Ball!" Gone is the frustration of the last place finish, replaced with an optimism brought on by a new lineup of players and the hope they bring. Winter is over; spring is here. We don't know exactly where we are going, but we are excited to begin the journey. Playoffs and championships are the focus of every player and every team.

Every day in the life of a Christ-follower should be a little like opening day. We never quite arrive, yet we get up every day with a single purpose, the upward call of God in Christ Jesus. With our focus on Jesus, we forget yesterday's failures and strive for the things the new day brings. We dwell in the hope, privileges, and responsibilities that come with the Christian life and the opportunities we have to worship and serve Him. It takes tremendous effort, but the prize is worth striving for. Each new day with Christ brings endless possibilities. We may not know exactly where we are going, but we should be excited about the journey. Stay focused; keep your eyes on the prize–Jesus Christ!

Father, I am excited about today because You are my focus. Teach me to put my yesterdays behind me and keep my eyes on the only prize worthy of pursuing–Your upward call in Christ Jesus. Amen.

Strength Through Weakness

"But He said to me, 'My grace is sufficient for you, for power is perfected in weakness.' Therefore, I will most gladly boast all the more about my weakness, so that Christ's power may reside in me. So because of Christ, I am pleased in weakness, in insults, in catastrophes, in persecutions, and in pressures. For when I am weak, then I am strong." 2 Corinthians 12:9-10

Our lives can change in an instant! Though we are consumed with our coaching responsibilities, life continues to happen around us. We tragically lose players and coaching friends to accidents or illness. In the middle of the season, we may lose a loved one or face the decision of placing a family member in assisted living. Out of nowhere, we are called into an administrator's office and told our contract will not be renewed. When these things happen, we are snatched back to the reality that there's little in life we control. Where do we turn when life gets rough? Where do we go when the pain seems to drain the life out of us?

Bad things happen, and we often ask God to take our pain and suffering away. That's not His way. But here's the good news; God promises His grace is all we need. We don't have to ask God to make His grace sufficient; it already is! In our times of greatest weakness and need, God is with us. Though none of us would volunteer to go through pain and suffering, we could probably agree we are closer to God during these times. The Apostle Paul is saying, if he is closer to Jesus in hard times, bring them on; he will gladly go through them. What about you? Are you going through a tough time right now? You have God's promise that His grace is enough to get you through, not over, not under and not around the tough times, but through them.

Father, thank You for Your love. We cling to Your promises as we go through the difficult times of life. When we are weak, You are strong. Teach us Lord, to draw closer to You when the times get tough. Amen.

What's in a Name?

"And whatever you do, in word and in deed, do everything in the name of the Lord Jesus, giving thanks to God the Father through Him." Colossians 3:17

Game planning is not the same for every opponent. Somewhere on every coach's schedule is a team that is not only talented but also has the reputation for being good over a long period. In Major League baseball it could be the New York Yankees or Los Angeles Dodgers. In the NBA, everyone still wants to beat the Los Angeles Lakers and Boston Celtics. Beating Alabama in college football or Connecticut in women's college basketball would look good on any team's resume. Not only do we have to get our players ready to play against the competition, but we must also prepare them to take on the reputation of the name itself. Just hearing the name Yankees, Celtics, Crimson Tide or Huskies can strike fear in an opponent's heart.

The name Jesus commands attention too! We struggle daily with difficult decisions. We are in constant battle over right and wrong. When making these decisions, we should ask ourselves the following questions. Can I do this in the name of the Lord Jesus Christ? Would this glorify Him? Would I want to be doing this when Jesus comes back again? Our answers could apply to the words we speak or the actions we take. To say we are doing something in the name of Jesus is powerful stuff! We had better be sure we mean it before we bring our Lord and Savior's name into the picture. There is no name more powerful and no name Satan fears more than that of Jesus! We have taken a major step toward obedience when we learn to do everything for the glory of His name.

Heavenly Father, I want to live for You, but I am weak. Help me understand that You are always there for me when I call Your name. Use me Lord, and I will give You the glory. Amen.

Champion or Chump?

"I know both how to have a little, and I know how to have a lot. In any and all circumstances I am." Philippians 4:12

The line between being a champion or a chump is very thin. Isn't it amazing that in one game, a coach can go from a genius to a complete idiot. The team that just won a big game is never going to lose again. The team that just fell apart is a bunch of bums who will never win again. The coaching roller coaster often takes us on a wild ride, and we have to be well grounded to keep things in the proper perspective. Here is a truth for you. It's seldom as good as it seems, nor as bad. Coaches will experience times of plenty as well as times of scarcity. Rarely in a season will we win them all or lose them all. Some years we have great talent, and other years we have little. The struggle for coaches is finding contentment in our process.

What does the Bible say about finding contentment? The Apostle Paul reminds us there is a secret to being content, and that secret is staying strong in Jesus. Contentment is the key in our witness for Jesus. How credible will our testimony be if we are only happy and content when things are going our way? Contentment with our situation in life reflects our faith and trust in Jesus Christ. If we continue reading Philippians 4:13, it says, "For I can do everything through Christ, who gives me strength." That strength is available in the good times and the bad. The great news is God continues to walk with us and stand beside us, regardless of what the world may think or say about us.

Lord, help me be content with all You have given me and help me do the best I can with it. Amen.

Keep Growing

"To the law and to the testimony! If they do not speak according to this word, there will be no dawn for them." Isaiah 8:20

Successful coaches are always learning! You can go to any clinic in the country and find the best coaches sitting on the front row. To me, that speaks volumes about why those coaches are successful. Successful coaches do not stand still; they're always looking for a nugget that can make them a better coach or team. There are also, however, coaches convinced they know all they need to know. They have their system; it has worked for years, so why look for ways to change. I have always liked the saying that past performance does not guarantee future success. My translation is that if you are standing still, it won't take long for someone to pass you.

I love spending time in God's Word, the Bible. Like the coach at a clinic, each time I open it up I find a nugget. I believe the more nuggets I can get and apply to my life, the better chance of success I will have in living out my life according to God's perfect plan. I want to stay hungry and be a lifelong learner when it comes to God's Word. I don't want to stand still or be in the dark. I want to be like those athletes who beg their coaches for more work. Being a student of the Bible does not guarantee success, but I do believe there will be fewer bumps along the way.

Heavenly Father, thank You for Your instruction book, the Bible. Grow me in knowledge and wisdom as I study and apply Your Word to my life today. Amen.

Represent

"Therefore, we are ambassadors for Christ; certain that God is appealing through us, we plead on Christ's behalf, 'Be reconciled to God.'" 2 Corinthians 5:20

As coaches, we often remind our athletes that they aren't just playing for themselves. It was a regular practice for me to tell my players that the name on the front of the uniform was more important than the name on the back. What I hoped to get across was the idea that as a team we represent much more. Each time we step on the field or court, we are being watched. People notice how we play as individuals and as a team. Opinions about our coaches, our school or club, and even our families are being formed as others observe our play. When time runs out, and the contest is over, how we respond in victory or defeat says a great deal about us. We should strive to be good ambassadors for our team, school, and community. Wouldn't it be great to hear opponents say, "I like playing the Falcons; they always play with real class!"

As followers of Jesus Christ, we must remember we represent someone greater than ourselves too. Jesus was the ultimate team player. No one served others better. No one sacrificed more. What a model to follow; what a responsibility we have to do all in our human strength to live up to the standard Jesus set. Every day people are watching us and how we go about our lives. Do we strive to be good ambassadors for Christ, or does our faith look like a roller coaster as we go through the ups and downs of life? What do people hear when we speak, and what do they see when they watch our actions? Wouldn't it be great if someone said to us, "There is something different about you; can we get together soon, so you can tell me more about this Jesus guy?"

Father God, thank You for Your Son Jesus. Help me understand others are watching me today. Guide my actions as I strive to be a worthy ambassador for You. Amen.

Better Than Average

"A thief comes only to steal and to kill and to destroy. I have come that they may have life and have it in abundance." John 10:10

Who wants to be an average athlete or coach? To truly compete means much more than to simply show up and participate. Great athletes and coaches have a deep desire to be the best. They put in the time and effort to improve their skills and knowledge of the game. I've heard it said that it takes 10,000 hours to become an expert at something. If I do the math, that's over four hundred days. Now I don't know if this number is fact or fiction, but what it does tell me is it takes a great deal of work. It also tells me why we have so few experts; most people will not put in the hours to be great. Those who dare to be great usually reap the rewards of their efforts whether it be fame, fortune or the self-satisfaction of being the best they could be.

The Apostle John knew Jesus well. Surely John watched and listened closely during the three-year ministry of his friend. To John and the other disciples, Jesus was anything but average. Jesus stood out in a crowd, and He wants that for us too. Jesus often referred to himself as the good shepherd, and he said his flock would follow him because they knew his voice. These followers, Jesus said, would find good pastures not average pastures. Jesus does not want you and me to settle for an average life; He wants the best for us. The amazing news is we can have this type of life immediately. Knowing that, why would we want anything less than the rich and full life He offers? Why would we hesitate?

Lord, average is not in Your vocabulary. Push me today to be all You have called me to be. Amen.

Finish Line

"Do you not know that the runners in a stadium all race, but only one receives the prize? Run in such a way that you may win. Now everyone who competes exercises self-control in everything. However, they do it to receive a perishable crown, but we an imperishable one." 1 Corinthians 9:24-25

All runners have one thing in mind—the finish line! I have enjoyed competing in some road races ranging from 5K's to marathons, and in each one, I have welcomed the finish. Regardless of the race distance, getting to the finish line requires certain things from participants. They must be prepared and focused. They must discipline themselves to follow a training schedule that prepares them to compete. They must focus on maintaining a constant and consistent pace throughout the entire race. There is nothing a runner fears more than the dreaded initials DNF (Did Not Finish) beside his/her name in the race results. Crossing the finish line means receiving the prize, usually a medal around your neck or the coveted race T-shirt.

Our Scripture is talking about another kind of race. We are reminded that our spiritual race will be challenging. To get to the finish line will require resolve, strength, courage, persistence, and tenacity. We must run with every ounce of energy we have. We will not finish the race if we are lazy and halfhearted. Paul speaks from experience because his race included persecution, hunger, beatings, homelessness and much more. Paul was able to endure because he was focused on the finish. He did not allow himself to get distracted, and he understood he was running for a prize much more precious than a medal that will tarnish or a T-shirt that will wear out. We, like Paul, are running for a prize that is priceless—eternal life. It is not a race for the faint of heart. Our challenge is to look at our spiritual race. Are we consistent or are we on-again-off-again? Do we know where we are going? Do we understand what it takes to get there? Run to win!

Heavenly Father, thank You for the race You have put me in. Help me run with focus and run my race to Win! Amen.